BY THE EDITORS OF
CONSUMER GUIDE®

PERENNIALS

A BEGINNER'S GUIDE TO
A COLORFUL GARDEN

Contributing Authors:
Carol Landa Christensen
Peter Loewer

Consultants:
Dr. Darrel Apps
Dr. Steven Still

Illustrator:
Mike Muir

Louis Weber, C.E.O.
Publications International, Ltd.
7373 North Cicero Avenue
Lincolnwood, IL 60646

Permission is never granted for commercial purposes.

Manufactured in the USA.

8 7 6 5 4 3 2 1

ISBN 1-56173-754-2

Photo Credits:

Steven M. Still: Front and back cover

Derek Fell: 36; **Steven M. Still:** 3, 4, 5, 6, 8, 12, 14, 16, 18, 20, 22, 26, 32, 34, 40, 42, 43, 44, 45, 46, 47, 48, 49, 50, 51, 52, 53, 54, 55, 56, 57, 58, 59, 60, 61, 62, 63, 64.

Contributing Authors:

Carol Landa Christensen graduated *cum laude* from the Pennsylvania School of Horticulture for Women, and went on to work at Longwood Gardens as a Horticultural Information Specialist and as a floral designer. She has written flower gardening features regularly for newspapers and *Gurney's Gardening News*.

Peter Loewer is a member of the Garden Writers Association of American and has written a number of books on gardening, including *Growing and Decorating with Grasses, American Gardens, The Annual Garden, Gardens by Design*, and *A Year of Flowers*.

Consultants:

Dr. Darrel Apps was the departmental Head of Education at Longwood Gardens for 12 years before he began his own consulting and training business, Garden Adventures. He is a frequent lecturer on horticultural topics and teaches courses on perennials.

Dr. Steven Still is a Professor of Horticulture at The Ohio State University and author of the widely used textbook, *Manual of Herbaceous Ornamental Plants*. Photographs from Dr. Still's extensive picture library appear frequently in many horticultural publications.

CONTENTS

Mixed gardens of perennials, annuals, and bulbs are very attractive.

Introduction

Foliage is just as important as flowers in a perennials garden.

Perennials are plants that survive winter outdoors to produce new growth and flowers each summer. Since they are not dug up and replanted each year, proper flower bed preparation is crucial. This book takes the beginning gardener through all the basic techniques. You'll learn how to prepare your soil and use the available light to best possible advantage. And since most perennials only bloom for two to three weeks, specific bloom dates are discussed.

It would be a mistake to place emphasis exclusively on perennial flowers. There is so much beauty in the textures and subtle colors of the foliage—just take a close look at bold hosta clumps in various shades of blue-green, green and white, and gold.

You'll also find tips for choosing the correct tools so that you can properly handle pregrown, potted, and bare-root plants. Also included are hints that tell you what to look for when selecting plants at the nursery, so that what you buy is healthy and in good condition.

Neither gardening chores, such as watering, weeding, and feeding, nor plant-staking techniques are difficult once you know how to do them. An illustrated section that allows easy identification of garden pests and diseases contains recommendations for dealing with each problem. Easy-to-follow information will help home gardeners successfully start plants from seed, from stem and root cuttings, and by various methods of division.

Because of the permanence of perennials, it pays to give advance consideration to where to plant them and which ones to use. You'll do some shifting and adjustments as you see the plantings develop, but you'll want to keep this to a minimum. To make the planning process easier, you'll learn how to lay out gardens on paper. Finally, the plant directory features descriptions, how-to-grow techniques, propagation, uses, and related varieties and species for at-a-glance information about the most common perennials.

Whether you use just a few perennials in bold masses among shrubs or under trees, mix them in with annuals, or specialize in the many varieties of one particular kind, you'll find that perennials provide dependable beauty year after year. And the more you know about perennials gardening, the more you'll learn to love it!

Planning for Lasting Color

Soil and Light

There are perennials suited to all garden conditions.

Soil and light are especially important factors when planning perennial planting. Along with water, they are the essential elements needed for successful gardening. We first need to know what kind of soil we have and to make any necessary adjustments, so it will be the best it can possibly be for growing plants. In the case of light, we must determine the amount that's available. With this information, we can make our plant selections: shade-loving plants for low-light areas; sun lovers for bright, sunny locations.

Let's talk about soil first. Soil types vary from the extremes of constantly dry, nutrient-poor sand to 90 percent rocks held together with 10 percent soil to rich, heavy clay (which forms a sticky, shoe-grabbing mass when wet, then dries to brick hardness). Fortunately, most soil conditions fall somewhere between these extremes. Still, very few homeowners find they have that ideal "rich garden loam" to work with!

Therefore, the first order of business is to learn just what kind of soil you *do* have. The way to do this is to have your soil tested. In some states, the county Cooperative Extension office will do soil-nutrient tests; in others, it's necessary to use the services of a private testing lab.

To obtain a representative sample of the soil in your flower bed, take a tablespoonful from each end of the bed and another from somewhere in the middle. Dig 4 to 6 inches down before taking each sample. Mix all of the samples together thoroughly in a single container. Then hand-carry or mail the mixture to those doing the testing.

You'll want a complete soil test. One part will be a pH test that reads for acidity and alkalinity. A pH test result between 6.0 and 7.0 is ideal and requires no adjustment. A result below 6.0 indicates the soil is too acid. Ground limestone should be added to correct this problem. If the reading is over 7.2, the soil is too alkaline. To solve this problem, add powdered sulfur or, for quicker results, iron sulfate.

In addition to pH, you'll receive information about the nutrients in your soil. If there is a deficiency in any of these nutrients, you'll need to add the missing elements as recommended in the report. A third result will tell you the percentage of organic materials your soil contains; this information will help you decide whether or not you need to supplement your soil with additional organic matter. (Details on fertilizing and improving garden soil can be found in the section "Watering, Weeding, and Feeding," page 20.)

Some homesites have so little soil or the soil is so poor that it cannot—or should not—be used at all. One solution in these situations is to build raised beds and fill them with high-quality soil brought in from elsewhere. Such beds should be at least 6 inches deep to allow good root penetration. This may seem a costly solution in the short-term, but the beds will last for years and prove themselves well worth your initial investment.

Another solution, especially in a small area, is to garden entirely in containers. An imaginative approach, such as installing a deck or patio over the useless ground and then decorating it with container-grown plants, can transform a sad eyesore into an oasis. (You'll find more details on container gardening on page 40.)

Light is another important factor in gardening. How much is there and for how many hours each day? In other words, does the area where you want to grow perennials have full sun, partial shade, or full shade?

At least to some extent, the amount of light the flower bed receives will dictate the plant species you'll be able to grow. Those plants that love full sun may become leggy and produce very few flowers if they're planted in a shady spot. By the same token, some plants are sensitive to too much light and will burn when placed in bright sunlight. Fortunately, there are perennials suited to all kinds of light conditions. Therefore, except for those places of deepest shade, there are many different kinds from which to choose.

Typical Soil Profile

A typical soil profile contains three basic layers: topsoil, subsoil, and bedrock. The depth of each of these layers varies tremendously. In New England alone, there are hilly areas where only 1 inch of topsoil and 1 inch of subsoil are found on top of the bedrock, while the nearby valleys have 15 inches of topsoil before subsoil is reached. Where there is insufficient topsoil, it is necessary to supplement it—perhaps in raised beds or behind a retaining wall—before perennials can be grown. Dig a straight-sided hole to see your soil profile.

Testing for Soil Type

Soil may vary from light sand to heavy clay. A rough test can be made by squeezing a wettened sample in your hand. If it falls apart easily, it's primarily sand; if it forms a solid, sticky glob, it's primarily clay. The ideal growing medium is somewhere between the two; by adding conditioners and humus to your soil, you can make it closer to that ideal. Send a soil sample to a testing lab to learn what additives and nutrients your soil needs.

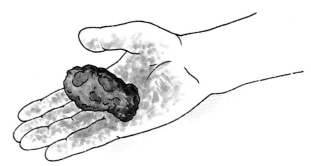

Color, Form, and Texture

Color, form, and texture are three very important characteristics that need to be considered when planning a perennials garden. They can make the difference between a garden that looks like it was thrown together and one that gives the impression of careful planning.

Color—The primary source of color is, of course, from flowers. But another equally important consideration is the color provided by existing backgrounds: fences, house walls, flowering shrubs, or the blossoms in neighboring gardens. If, for example, the background is painted white, white flowers planted against it will become virtually invisible. If the background contains bright red flowers, you may not want the vivid contrast that purple blooms would add. If the area is backed by dark woods or evergreens, you should keep in mind that dark shades of blue and purple will disappear; whites, yellows, silver-grays, and yellow-greens will stand out.

In addition to such physical considerations, there are also emotional ones: Color can be mood setting. Red, yellow, and orange shades are bright, warm, and cheering. On the other hand, blues, silvers, and whites are calming and cooling—they can be very soothing during the heat of summer. A nostalgic, romantic look can be achieved by using pale pastels; a modern, upbeat style results when pure bright colors are mixed. Think about the mood and atmosphere you'd like to create in each area of your garden; it may differ from one location to another and even from one season to the next.

Two hints on color: 1) White flowers will blend easily with any other colors you select; and 2) If you vary the intensity of different flower colors in your design, you can often help add vitality and interest to the planting.

Form and Texture—Plant form and texture are especially important aspects of perennials because, for a good part of the growing season when they're not in bloom, that's all that is to be enjoyed of these plants. In fact, in the case of some perennials, form and texture are *all* that matters: Fern clumps take us from the early spring unfolding of their fiddleheads through the fully open filigree of their fronds and on to their golden autumn color. Flowers are not utilized for this effect at all. Many hostas and stonecrops are also better known for their foliage effects than for their flowers.

An extra bonus to be savored and utilized in the landscape is a plant that has lovely blossoms as well

Contrast in color, form, and texture can be very pleasing.

as an attractive growth habit. The flowers themselves vary in form and texture, too: the huge, airy clouds of baby's breath; tall, handsome spires of delphiniums; the round pompoms of chrysanthemums and peonies; and the graceful arches of bleeding hearts—each bloom perfectly heart-shaped.

Among perennials, there are some outstandingly handsome examples of foliage and form. Peonies have a rugged, bold leaf cluster that turns to wonderful shades of pink or bronze in the autumn; hostas provide dramatic low clumps that can be used alone or combined with other plants; and the blue-gray globe thistle foliage makes a handsome bush.

Fortunately, many perennials offer this added bonus of interesting texture and/or form to the garden. In many instances, they also offer a color contrast as well. Use plants with these bonuses wherever possible, although it doesn't mean you should completely bypass those that only have attractive blooms to their credit. Instead, intermix the outstanding stars with the duller kinds. You'll produce a complete planting, which is interesting throughout the growing season—whether in bloom or not.

The Varied Forms of Perennials

The form, or shape, of perennials is important to consider when designing a garden. By selecting plants with varying forms, the garden will be more interesting to look at.

Ground-hugging

Arching

Rounded

Textures of Perennials

A variety of textures adds to a garden's beauty. Placing plants with feathery foliage or flowers next to ones with coarse, bold characteristics will produce a dramatic-looking garden.

Feathering

Coarse & Bold

9

Selecting Perennials for Color and Characteristics

These charts provide a quick reference for selecting plants for your garden. When scanning these lists, you may find many plants that seem appropriate. However, on further investigation, you'll find that many of them won't work after all. Use the charts to narrow down your choices; then refer to the more detailed description in the directory section to identify those best suited to your climate, soil, and light conditions.

It's important to remember that the "Multicolor" category lists those plants that come in nearly every color range (any perennial that comes in more than three color ranges has been put into this category). Because it contains the most universal and versatile perennials, be sure to use it often when making your selections.

MULTICOLOR

	Dry Soil	Average Soil	Moist Soil	Full Sun	Part Shade	Full Shade	Under 12 Inches	12–24 Inches	Over 24 Inches	Vining
Astilbe; Garden Spiraea		•	•	•				•	•	
Balloon Flower	•	•	•	•				•	•	
Bergamot; Bee-Balm; Oswego-Tea		•	•	•						•
Bergenia, Heartleaf		•			•			•		
Chrysanthemum		•		•				•	•	
Columbine		•		•	•			•	•	
Coralbell; Alumroot	•	•		•	•			•		
Crane's-Bill	•			•	•		•	•		
Daisy, Michaelmas	•			•		•	•	•		
Daylily	•	•	•	•				•	•	
Delphinium; Larkspur	•	•	•						•	
Indigo, False; Wild Indigo	•	•		•	•				•	
Iris		•	•	•			•	•	•	
Lungwort; Jerusalem Sage		•			•	•		•		
Lupine		•	•	•					•	
Peony		•	•	•	•				•	
Phlox, Garden		•		•	•				•	
Pink; Carnation		•		•			•	•		
Poppy		•		•					•	
Speedwell		•		•	•			•		
Spiderwort		•		•	•			•		
Stonecrop	•	•		•			•	•		
Yarrow	•	•		•	•			•	•	

BLUE TO PURPLE

	Dry Soil	Average Soil	Moist Soil	Full Sun	Part Shade	Full Shade	Under 12 Inches	12–24 Inches	Over 24 Inches	Vining
Bellflower		•	•	•	•		•	•	•	
Bugleweed		•		•	•		•			
Bugloss, Siberian		•	•	•	•		•			
Coneflower, Purple		•		•					•	
Hosta; Plantain Lily	•	•	•		•	•		•	•	
Lavender	•	•		•				•		
Rockcress	•	•		•	•		•			
Thistle, Globe	•	•		•	•				•	

RED

	Dry Soil	Average Soil	Moist Soil	Full Sun	Part Shade	Full Shade	Under 12 Inches	12–24 Inches	Over 24 Inches	Vining
Avens		•	•	•				•		
Blanket Flower		•		•				•		

PINK TO FUCHSIA

	Dry Soil	Average Soil	Moist Soil	Full Sun	Part Shade	Full Shade	Under 12 Inches	12–24 Inches	Over 24 Inches	Vining
Anemone, Japanese		•	•	•	•				•	
Baby's Breath		•		•			•	•	•	
Bleeding Heart			•		•			•		
Coneflower, Purple		•		•					•	
Obedient Plant; False-Dragonhead		•	•	•				•	•	
Rockcress	•	•		•	•		•			
Rose, Christmas; Lenten Rose; Hellebore			•		•				•	

YELLOW TO ORANGE

	Dry Soil	Average Soil	Moist Soil	Full Sun	Part Shade	Full Shade	Under 12 Inches	12–24 Inches	Over 24 Inches	Vining
Avens	•	•	•					•		
Basket-of-Gold; Goldentuft; Madwort; Gold-Dust	•		•		•					
Blanket Flower	•		•					•		
Coneflower, Yellow; Black-Eyed Susan	•	•	•						•	
Coreopsis	•		•				•	•	•	
Lady's Mantle	•	•	•	•				•		
Leopard's-Bane	•	•		•				•		
Ligularia			•		•				•	
Sneezeweed		•	•						•	

GRASSES & FOLIAGE

	Dry Soil	Average Soil	Moist Soil	Full Sun	Part Shade	Full Shade	Under 12 Inches	12–24 Inches	Over 24 Inches	Vining
Bugleweed		•		•	•	•				
Hosta		•	•	•	•	•		•	•	
Stonecrop	•	•		•			•	•		
Wormwood	•	•		•					•	

WHITE TO GREEN

	Dry Soil	Average Soil	Moist Soil	Full Sun	Part Shade	Full Shade	Under 12 Inches	12–24 Inches	Over 24 Inches	Vining
Anemone, Japanese	•	•	•	•					•	
Baby's Breath	•			•			•	•	•	
Bellflower	•	•	•	•			•	•	•	
Bleeding Heart		•			•			•		
Bugleweed	•			•	•		•			
Candytuft	•			•			•			
Coneflower, Purple	•	•							•	
Hosta; Plantain Lily	•	•	•	•	•	•		•	•	
Obedient Plant; False-Dragonhead	•	•	•					•	•	
Rose, Christmas; Lenten Rose; Hellebore		•			•			•		

These cultural recommendations are intended to suggest the average conditions over a widespread geographical area. It is important to be aware of local requirements.

Sequence of Bloom

Because individual perennials have a limited season of bloom, it's important to know when you can expect each of them to flower. If you want color throughout the entire growing season, you'll need to plan on a succession of bloom provided by different species. With proper planning, it's possible to do this entirely with perennials, even though perennials don't have to stand alone. To obtain summer-long bloom, it's possible to intermix annuals with perennials—the annuals will provide additional flower color from mid-summer to late summer.

Also remember that perennial and annual bulbs offer additional summer color possibilities. Gladioli, tuberoses, fritillarias, resurrection lilies, and, in warm climates, creeping buttercups, can be tucked into small spaces between other plants to provide additional color. Most varied and beautiful are the many hardy lilies that provide an outstanding display of different colors and forms throughout the summer.

Most perennials bloom gloriously at some point during the growing season.

Summer isn't the only season when bulbs add beauty to the landscape. All of the spring-flowering bulbs—tulips, daffodils, flowering onions, crocuses, scillas, snowdrops, hyacinths, anemones, etc.—are certainly well known, popular, and easily grown perennial additions to most gardens.

Selecting Perennials by Bloom Date

This bloom date chart is designed for Zone 7 (see map on pages 30-31). Bloom time is approximately 10-14 days earlier for each zone south and 10-14 days later for each zone north for each given entry.

EARLY SPRING	
February-March	
Rose, Christmas; Lenten Rose; Hellebore	*Helleborus* species

LATE SPRING	
April-May	
Avens	*Geum* species

LATE SPRING (continued)	
April-May	
Basket-of-Gold; Goldentuft; Madwort; Gold-Dust	*Aurinia saxatilis*
Bergenia, Heartleaf	*Bergenia cordifolia*
Bleeding Heart	*Dicentra* species
Candytuft	*Iberis sempervirens*
Columbine	*Aquilegia* species
Coralbell; Alumroot	*Heuchera sanguinea*
Crane's-Bill	*Geranium* species
Indigo, False; Wild Indigo	*Baptisia australis*
Iris	*Iris* species
Lady's Mantle	*Alchemilla* species
Leopard's-Bane	*Doronicum cordatum*

LATE SPRING (continued)
April-May

Lungwort; Jerusalem Sage	*Pulmonaria officinalis*
Peony	*Paeonia* species
Pink; Carnation	*Dianthus* species
Poppy	*Papaver orientale*
Rockcress	*Aubrieta deltoidea*

SUMMER
June-August

Anemone, Japanese	*Anemone* species
Astilbe; Garden Spiraea	*Astilbe* species
Avens	*Geum* species
Baby's Breath	*Gypsophila paniculata*
Balloon Flower	*Platycodon grandiflorus*
Bellflower	*Campanula* species
Bergamot; Bee-Balm; Oswego-Tea	*Monarda didyma*
Blanket Flower	*Gaillardia* x *grandiflora*
Bleeding Heart	*Dicentra* species
Coneflower, Yellow; Black-Eyed Susan	*Rudbeckia fulgida*
Coralbell; Alumroot	*Heuchera sanguinea*
Coreopsis	*Coreopsis* species
Crane's-Bill	*Geranium* species
Daisy, Michaelmas	*Aster* species
Daylily	*Hemerocallis* species
Delphinium; Larkspur	*Delphinium* species
Iris	*Iris* species

SUMMER (continued)
June-August

Lavender	*Lavandula angustifolia*
Ligularia	*Ligularia* species
Lupine	*Lupinus polyphyllus*
Obedient Plant; False-Dragonhead	*Physostegia virginiana*
Phlox, Garden	*Phlox paniculata*
Sneezeweed; Swamp Sunflower	*Helenium autumnale*
Speedwell	*Veronica spicata*
Spiderwort	*Tradescantia* x *Andersoniana*
Thistle, Globe	*Echinops ritro*
Wormwood	*Artemisia* species
Yarrow	*Achillea* species

FALL
September-Frost

Anemone, Japanese	*Anemone* species
Bleeding Heart	*Dicentra* species
Chrysanthemum	*Chrysanthemum* species
Coralbell; Alumroot	*Heuchera sanguinea*
Coreopsis	*Coreopsis* species
Daisy, Michaelmas	*Aster* species
Obedient Plant; False-Dragonhead	*Physostegia virginiana*
Sneezeweed; Swamp Sunflower	*Helenium autumnale*
Speedwell	*Veronica spicata*
Stonecrop	*Sedum spectabile*
Wormwood	*Artemisia* species

Getting Your Garden Off to a Good Start

Groundwork: Turning and Enriching the Earth

A well-prepared garden bed ensures healthy plant growth.

I f the results of your soil test indicate a lack of certain nutrients, you should follow the recommendations made by the testing company. If the imbalance is slight, organic fertilizers can be used. When fast results are needed, or if the imbalance of nutrients is great, inorganic fertilizers are the better choice. A combination of both may be a good compromise solution, using the quick-to-feed commercial plant foods first, then following up in subsequent years with the slow-feeding organic fertilizers.

Commercial fertilizer is commonly formulated in some combination of the three major nutrients: nitrogen, phosphorus, and potassium—N,P,K. The numbers featured on each bag represent the percentage of each of these nutrients in the mix. For example, a 5-10-5 mixture contains 5 percent nitrogen (N), 10 percent phosphorus (P), and 5 percent potassium (K). A mixture of 10-10-10 contains 10 percent of each. The NPK formula is also listed on each container of organic fertilizer. The percentages of each nutrient are lower in organic fertilizers than in inorganics. Larger amounts of organics are required to achieve the same results.

It's possible to purchase nutrients separately rather than in a three-nutrient mix. These are useful when there's a deficiency in a single nutrient. Consult with your county Cooperative Extension office or garden center if you feel uncertain about solving nutrient deficiency problems.

Adjusting the nutrient and pH levels in your soil will not improve its *consistency*. To correct soil texture will require the addition of one or several "soil conditioners." The most commonly used conditioners are leaf mold, compost, well-rotted cow manure, and peat moss. Vermiculite, perlite, and sand (coarse builder's sand, *never* use beach sand) can also be added, especially when the basic soil is heavy.

After preparing a planting bed, allow the soil to stand unplanted for a week or more. Stir the surface inch or two every three to four days with a rake to eradicate fast-germinating weed seeds. This will make your future weeding chores lighter.

This is also the time to install some kind of mowing strip. Patio squares or slate pieces laid end-to-end at ground level will keep grass and flowers from intermixing. Other options include landscape logs, poured concrete strips, or bricks laid side-by-side on a sand or concrete base. The mowing strip must be deep and wide enough so grass roots cannot tunnel underneath or travel across the top to reach the flower bed, and the top of the strip must not extend above the level of the adjacent lawn.

Preparing a Garden Bed

1 Mark out the new garden area with pegs and string as guides for digging (use a garden hose as a guide for any curved lines). Using a spade or edger, cut through the sod along string lines, skim the sod layer off, then cut back and remove any underlying roots.

2 Thoroughly turn and loosen the soil to about a 6-inch depth, removing rocks as you go. For medium to large areas, use a Rototiller for this job (if you don't have one, either rent one or hire someone to do the tilling). For a very small area, use a spade.

3 Smooth the soil surface with an iron rake—do a very rough job, since you'll be redigging the area again. Remove rocks and roots that surface during the raking.

4 Spread on soil additives (compost, moistened peat moss, perlite, fertilizer, etc.) as recommended by your soil test results. Work them in with a tiller or spade—since the upper soil layer is much looser, you'll be able to till more deeply—to a 10- to 12-inch depth—this second time. Wait a week or so before planting in order to allow the soil to settle.

Potted Perennials

Most potted plants are healthy and strong.

Although most garden centers try very hard to supply healthy plants in peak condition—free of disease and insect infestations—it's still possible for problems to escape their notice. A reputable retailer will certainly replace any plants that you may purchase and find to be sick after getting them home. However, by then the damage of passing the problem on to other plants in your garden may already have been done. It is far better to learn what to look for, so that you can protect yourself as much as possible from this kind of problem!

First and foremost, observe the degree of care or neglect that the plants receive at each nursery or garden center. If plants appear wilted, leaves are sun-scorched, or the soil is bone dry, it's probably not a one-time happening. Each time a plant wilts badly, it loses strength. If the retailer doesn't water regularly and does not provide shade for the more vulnerable and shade-loving plants, it's very likely that the plants will be in a weakened condition when you buy them. This, in turn, makes them more susceptible to disease and insect infestations, because they have less strength with which to survive such problems.

Unless you buy the plants very early in the season before they've gone through many wilting cycles, it's best not to purchase plants from a source where they haven't received proper care. There are many alternative sources where good care is given. Always look for strong, vital, healthy new growth and plants that have been handled properly.

You also want to inspect each plant carefully for signs of infestation. Signs of problems include: stippled holes dotting leaves (leafhoppers); squiggly trails on leaves (leaf miners); extremely fine webs on underside of leaves (red spiders); stickiness on plant stems and leaves (red spiders or aphids); colonies of tiny, soft-bodied bugs on flower buds and growth tips (aphids); ants busily running up and down stems (aphids); whitish fluff that turns sticky if pinched (mealybugs); hard, round or oval, shell-like formations on stems (scale); cloud of tiny white insects rising from the plant when you touch it (white flies); leaf edges chewed (caterpillars); grayish-white powder on leaves (mildew); and plant tips wilted, while lower stems and leaves are not (stem borers). More detailed descriptions of insects and diseases can be found on page 26; this list simply provides the primary warning signals to heed when screening plants in the garden center. If you think you see any of these signals, point them out to your retailer. Especially during their busy spring season, it's difficult for retailers to spot the beginning of every possible problem. Good plantsmen will want to take steps to combat an infestation as early as possible.

Many garden shops and nurseries offer an extensive variety of perennials planted in containers. Whereas in the past there were just a few mail-order specialists from whom the more unusual perennials could be purchased, it's now possible to obtain what you want locally. This allows you to select the individual plants you prefer and to see their condition before you buy.

Potted perennials are offered in a number of sizes from small plants in 3- to 4-inch pots to mature plants in gallon-sized, metal or plastic containers. The small plants are usually only a few months old. In most instances, these will not produce blooms the first season. Those in large containers are often in bloom at the time of purchase and can be expected to quickly become established in their new sites. Smaller plants usually cost less than larger ones; when small plants are priced high, it's because they're rare or exceedingly slow or difficult to propagate.

Containerized plants should be planted outdoors as promptly as possible after purchase. The longer they're kept in containers, the more likely they are to dry out and become pot-bound. If you *must* hold plants for a long time prior to planting, place them where they'll be under light shade, and be sure to water them.

When you're ready to plant container-grown plants, thoroughly moisten the soil before knocking them out of the pot. Plunge the container into a pail of water to above the pot's rim for a few minutes. Snap off any roots sticking out of the pot bottom. The plant should slide out into your hand. If it doesn't, run a knife blade around the inside of the pot to help release the root ball. If all else fails, break off the pot by knocking it against something solid; in the case of plastic or metal containers, cut them open and peel them off, avoiding damage to the roots as much as is reasonably possible.

Loosen and remove any excess soil from around the roots. Most soilless mixes will fall away on their own. If the mix adheres to the roots, take away only as much as comes off easily with your fingers. Soilless mixes dry faster than garden soil, so you want to eliminate what you can without badly disturbing the root ball.

Always place the plant in the ground at the same depth as it was in the pot and provide a water-holding area by forming a soil dam a few inches away from the stem. Transplant in the evening or on a cloudy day; otherwise, provide shade for three to four days by setting an overturned box or a newspaper cone over each plant. Tuck a 2-inch mulch layer around the plants and deep-water as needed the first growing season. Remember that good care is the key to success!

Transplanting Potted Plants

1 Submerge potted plants in water before transplanting; this helps the plant to slide out of the container more easily. To avoid damage to the plant top and help keep the root ball intact, spread your hand over the top of the pot with stems and leaves poking out between your fingers. Then turn the pot upside down and gently tap its rim against something solid to loosen the root ball from the sides of the pot. The plant will slide out of the pot into your hand.

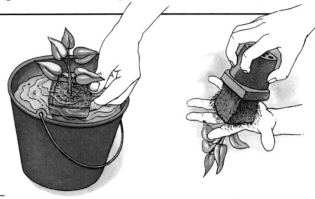

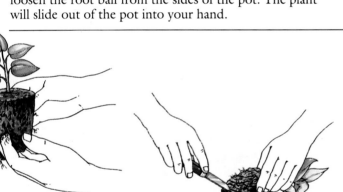

2 If the plant root ball is tightly packed with roots, these should be gently loosened. They need to spread out after planting, rather than continue to grow in a tight mass. If they resist loosening with your fingers, cut up into the sides of the root ball in several places with a sharp knife or scissors, then shake the roots loose a bit more with your fingers before planting. If roots are not tightly packed, skip this step. *Note:* Knock only one plant out at a time to avoid exposing the roots to the drying qualities of air and light.

3 The plant hole should be somewhat larger in diameter than the root ball and deep enough to allow you to plant at the same depth as when the plant was growing in the container. Fan out the loosened roots over a small soil mound in the center of the hole to encourage spreading root growth.

4 Refill the hole with soil, then firm the soil around the plant stem and roots. Create a soil dam around the plant and fill it with water. As the water soaks in, it will help settle the soil and remove any remaining air pockets around the roots—air pockets can cause delicate feeder roots to dry out and die. Lay a 2-inch layer of mulch around the crown and under trailing foliage.

Setting Bare-Root Plants

T he term "bare-root" is self-explanatory: There is *no* soil around the plant roots when you unpack the plant, although there is often a bit of moist excelsior packing. Plants sent by mail order are usually packed bare-root; you can also occasionally find perennials in garden centers that are packed this way.

This technique of packing works perfectly well and is in no way harmful to the plants, as long as the roots have remained moist in transit. If you find the roots are bone dry when you receive your shipment, there is some cause for concern. If this happens, thoroughly soak the plant roots immediately, then plant them outdoors after they've had an hour or so to take up water. Most will revitalize; report any that don't show signs of new growth after three weeks, explaining the dry condition upon arrival. Plant-supply houses are so experienced in packing bare-root plants that there is seldom a problem; when there is, it's usually because the shipment was somehow delayed in transit.

Ideally, bare-root plants should be planted immediately. If that's impossible, unpack them right away and place their roots in a container of water (do not submerge the tops). The sooner they're planted, the less energy they lose. If you must delay planting, pot the plants in containers and grow them as potted plants until you're ready to plant them in the ground.

Most perennials are best transplanted in the spring or, as a second choice, in the fall. Bearded irises, oriental poppies, and peonies usually fare better if moved only in the fall. The best planting periods for bare-root plants are: Northeast coast, spring and early to late fall; inland Northeast, spring and early fall; middle-Atlantic coast, mid- to late fall; Southeast, mid- to late fall and early spring; Midwest, spring and late summer to early fall; the Plains, spring and early to mid-fall; eastern side of the Rockies, spring; Pacific Northwest coast, early spring and fall; California, early spring and mid- to late fall; and the Southwest, early to mid-spring.

Place bare-root plants at the same depth as in the nursery—look for the soil line on the stem as a guide. However, those that arrive as dormant roots have no stems or top growth as indicators. The depths at which to plant these types are: oriental poppy—top of root 2 to 3 inches below soil surface; peony—lay root flat with top of clump 1 inch below soil surface; bearded iris—lay flat with top of clump right at, or very slightly above, the soil surface.

When planting bare-root plants, don't just dig a small hole and jam the roots into it. Make the hole large enough so you can carefully spread the roots out in all directions. Aftercare is the same as for containerized plants from this stage onward.

Bearded irises are best transplanted in the spring or fall.

Planting Bare-Root Plants

1 Unpack bare-root plants as soon as they arrive, planting them as quickly as possible. Always keep the roots moist and away from the wind and sun—they don't have any soil around them to help protect their feeder roots from drying out! Trim any extra long or damaged roots with sharp scissors before planting. Inspect, trim, and plant one plant at a time to avoid extended exposure to air and sun.

2 Set the plant in the hole so the soil line on the plant is at the same level as it was in the nursery. Spread out the roots evenly over a soil mound to help encourage well-rounded root growth.

3 Fill in the soil firmly around the roots, then fill the dam with water, and mulch. Provide shade to the new transplant for one day with an overturned box, newspaper cone, or similar shading.

Giving Your Perennials Lots of Care

Watering, Weeding, and Feeding

Deep-watering encourages strong root formation.

I f you feed and water perennials well and keep weeds from intruding on their space, they'll respond with vigorous growth and numerous blooms. Here's how to keep them at their best:

Watering—Water, soil, and sun are the most essential ingredients for plants. It's necessary to water perennials the first season after planting, whenever nature doesn't supply enough rain. After the first year, most perennials can sustain themselves without watering, except during exceptionally dry spells.

When watering *is* necessary, always water deeply in order to encourage deep root growth. When only the surface inch or two is moistened, the plant's roots are encouraged to grow primarily in that area. Then, as soon as the soil surface dries, they quickly wilt. Shallow-rooted plants are also not anchored well enough to survive strong winds or winter's freezing and thawing action.

Deep-watering is done most easily, and is least wasteful of water, when applied with a soaker hose laid around the plants. Allow water to slowly seep from the hose into the soil over a period of several hours. Dig down into the soil to be sure it has soaked in to a depth of 6 to 8 inches. Don't water again until a bit of soil pinched between your fingers feels nearly dry.

Weeding—Mulching helps retain soil moisture. It also greatly reduces the need for weeding, because the mulch layer inhibits many weed seeds from sprouting. Lay on the mulch to a depth of 2 inches right after planting. As you spread the mulch, take care to lift trailing foliage so it lies on top of the mulch, and be sure to keep space open around each plant's growth center to avoid smothering.

When a mulch is used, only a bit of hand weeding will be required around perennials. However, if for some reason a mulch is not used, hand cultivation of the top 1 inch of soil will be needed fre-quently throughout the summer to stir up the soil and discourage weed growth. Care must be taken not to damage roots or leave them exposed to sun and air, and not to scratch so deeply that hidden bulbs are damaged.

A third alternative for weed control among perennials is to sprinkle a pre-emergent chemical weed control on the soil between the plants. This should not be used in areas where seeds or young plants are growing; once plants are 4 to 6 inches high, they will not be harmed by these chemicals.

Feeding—Perennials profit from two or three light applications of general fertilizer each summer. Most important is a sidedressing of granular fertilizer each spring as growth starts; one or two additional lighter applications at 3- to 4-week intervals are helpful but not essential.

Use a commercial mixture of 5-10-5 or 10-10-10. If you prefer to use an organic fertilizer, simply apply more heavily, or at more frequent intervals to supply the same level of nutrition to the plants.

Watering with a Soaker Hose

A soaker hose allows water to slowly seep into the soil, allowing deep, thorough watering. At the same time, it applies water directly to the root zone without waste in runoff.

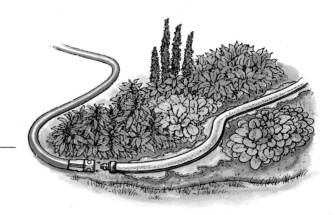

Sidedressing

Granular fertilizer is applied by sprinkling it over the root zone of each plant—this is known as sidedressing—taking care to avoid contact with the foliage. Apply just before a rainfall, or water after application, in order to start the feeding process.

Mulching

A mulch layer on top of the soil keeps down weeds, almost entirely eliminating the need for weeding. It helps retain moisture in the soil, reducing the need for watering, and gives the garden a neat, cared-for appearance.

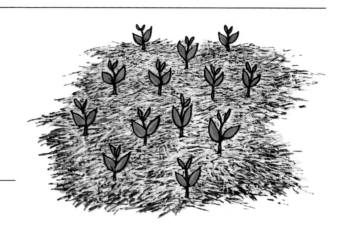

Feeding with Foliar Fertilizers

Plants are capable of absorbing nutrients through their foliage as well as their roots. A way to supply fertilizer quickly is by spraying it directly onto the plant foliage with a sprayer, watering can, or hose feeding attachment. Buy foliar fertilizers that are specially formulated for this purpose, following the manufacturer's instructions carefully to avoid burning of the foliage.

Hand Weeding

When a mulch is used, very little weeding is required—simply pull out the few weeds that are present by hand. Without a mulch, there will be more weeds to control; stir the top 1 to 2 inches of soil with a hand cultivator frequently to kill young weed seedlings as they emerge. Use a weeding tool to root them if they are larger and better established.

Ways to Increase/Control Growth

As has already been described, perennials will flourish when provided with the best possible growing conditions. However, there are a few simple care techniques that will help increase and control their growth.

Pinching Back—To encourage plants to fill out, remove the growth bud at the end of the main stem when the plant is in the rapid growth stage that precedes flower bud formation. Simply pinch out or snap off the last 1 inch or so of the main growing tip. This will redirect the plant's energy from this single shoot to numerous latent side buds—there is a latent growth bud located at the point on the stem where each leaf is attached.

Several days after pinching, you'll see small side shoots pushing from the remaining stem. These will grow into a cluster of stems to replace the original single stem. The plant will be shorter, stockier, and fuller than if no pinching had been done. It will also be neater looking, more compact, and have many more branches on which to produce flowers.

A second pinching can be done two weeks after the first if an even fuller plant is wanted. Pinching is not right for *all* perennials. Chrysanthemums, for example, respond well to pinching.

Disbudding—If you want to have each stem produce a single large bloom rather than numerous smaller ones, it's possible to steer all of the plant's energy into one terminal bud by snapping out all side buds along the stem as they appear. Disbudding is often done on peonies and oriental poppies.

Deadheading—There are two reasons for removing spent flowers promptly: 1) Once the flower dies, it detracts from the good looks of the garden; and 2) Even though we say it's dead, it's actually very much alive and continues with its growth toward seed production. This process pulls plant energy into the seed head that would otherwise be available for foliage and root production.

Shearing—The abundance of dead flower heads on low-spreading plants is most easily removed by shearing them with grass clippers immediately after they've finished blooming. This shearing of the top few inches will not only speedily dispose of unwanted dead blooms, but will also encourage attractive new foliage growth.

Pruning Back—Occasionally, it becomes necessary to cut back growth in order to keep a plant

These slender-stemmed delphiniums often require staking.

from drowning out neighboring plants. Cut back to a side bud or shoot that is headed in the direction you want future growth to go. In the case of grasses and other plants that grow from a ground level central crown, cut back the entire stem.

Although many perennials are sturdy and self-supporting, some plants with flower clusters on top of tall slender stems, such as lilies and delphiniums, may flop over when there are strong winds or heavy rains. Another group that sometimes requires support to keep flower heads visible are those with weak stems, which will either bend over or break off when the weight of their leaves and blooms becomes too great. Some varieties of peonies and bearded irises are known to have these problems.

Often plants gain enough support when a sort of corral is placed around them. The plant stems lean out against the metal or string sides of the corral instead of flopping down to the ground.

Another simple type of support consists of poking many-branched pieces of brush into the ground beside the plants. These form a network of twigs through which the plants can grow and against which they can lean for support. For greater support, the tops of these branches can be bent over to form an interlaced network.

The above support systems work well for plants with a spreading growth habit. For those that produce tall, single spikes, a third staking method is suitable. Two or three inches from the plant stem, poke a wooden or bamboo stake into the ground. Push it in deeply enough so it's solidly secure. Loosely tie each plant stem to this central stake every 6 inches along the stem's height. The topmost tie should be just below the flower bud cluster. To keep the ties from sliding down, first form a half-granny knot around the stake, then a full-granny knot around the plant stem.

Sometimes tying plants seems a nuisance, although it really only takes a few minutes to do.

But if those plants that need it aren't tied, they'll either bend over, becoming impossible to see; or they'll snap off, wilt, and die. If you aren't willing to stake your plants, then don't grow those that require it. Select easier-care varieties instead—there are many with sturdy growth habits that don't need staking.

Of course, if it happens that your favorite plant is one that needs staking, you'll probably conclude you like it enough to give it this bit of extra care in return for the pleasure and beauty it will provide.

Increasing Growth Through Pinching

Pinching out the growth tip early in the season encourages plants such as chrysanthemums and asters to push out multiple side shoots. This creates a fuller and more spreading plant with many more flower buds than if it were left unpinched.

Shearing Low-Spreading Plants

Some perennials can be sheared to remove dead flowers. This is particularly useful on low-spreading plants, which are literally covered with flowers each spring. Shearing should be done immediately after the flowers have faded to encourage the plant to fill out and look attractive the rest of the season as well as to produce abundant blooms the following year.

Deadheading

Deadheading, or the removal of dead flower heads, should be done soon after the flower dies so no plant energy is wasted on seed formation. Cut the flower off at a point just above a side shoot or branch, or down to the ground if the plant pushes flowers directly from the root crown.

Thinning

Some plants such as phlox, aster, and delphinium produce so much foliage that none of it blooms well. By thinning out all but a few of the strongest shoots in early spring, it's possible to channel the plant energy into these to produce nice, large blooms. To do this, use a sharp knife, scissors, or hand pruners to cut out all but the sturdiest half dozen stems when they reach a height of 4 to 6 inches. The remaining stalks will quickly fill in the spaces and prosper without the excess competition.

Brush Thicket Staking

A simple, no-cost plant support for fine-stemmed perennials can be made by poking the stems of well-branched brush into the ground around the plants in early spring. The plants' stems simply lean against the twigs for support, without any tying. Even more support can be gained from this brush thicket if the tops are bent over and interwoven.

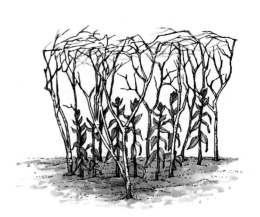

Corral Staking

Another good way to hold clumps of stems upright is by inserting four or more plant stakes around each plant. Tie a string around one stake, then wrap it one turn around each of the other stakes and back to the starter stake. For a large clump, run strings diagonally across within the corral that has been formed to provide even more of a support network. Several tiers of string, spaced 4 to 6 inches apart, may be needed for tall plants. The flower heads should float 6 to 8 inches above the top tier of strings.

L-Shaped Metal Stakes

A more expensive but easier to install corral can be made from L-shaped metal stakes sold especially for this purpose. These stakes hook together quickly to make whatever size is needed. These can be used year after year once the initial investment is made. String can be diagonally cross-woven between these stakes if more support is needed.

Individual Staking

Those plants that have tall individual stems are best staked individually. Push a tall stake deeply into the soil about 6 inches out from the stem base so it's firmly anchored. Tie the string to the stake first with a half-granny knot, then around the plant stem with a full-granny knot. Leave 1 inch or more of slack between the stake and the stem. As the plant grows taller, add ties further up the stalk—6 to 8 inches apart. The topmost tie should be located at the base of the flower spike.

Woven Wire Support

A plant support made from woven wire that is coated with green plastic is inconspicuous and effective. Supports can be either dome-shaped or an open topped circle. Placed over plants in early spring, they support the plants as the shoots grow up through them, ultimately covering them up completely.

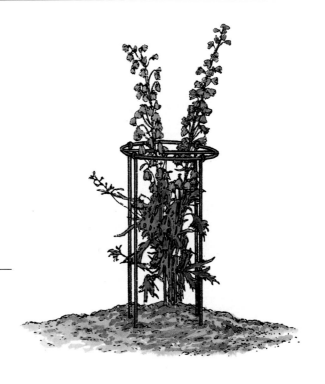

Pests and Other Problems

Healthy looking plants are a gardener's reward.

The following lists are designed to help you identify the most common garden pests and diseases. Once you know what your problem is, you'll need to decide how to control it. When an infestation is slight, it's often possible to simply remove the sick plants or individual insects. For a heavy infestation, you'll probably need to turn to chemical insecticides or fungicides. Our charts present both forms of treatment, distinguishing which are organic and which are inorganic.

INSECTS AND ANIMALS

SYMPTOM	CAUSE	CURE	PLANTS
Cluster of small, soft-bodied insects on buds and growth tips (gray, black, pink, or green in color); sticky secretions may be evident	Aphids	Spray with rotenone or malathion[1] in evening.	Chrysanthemum Delphinium Lupine
Leaves chewed away; hard-shelled beetles on plant and burrowed into flowers	Beetles of various kinds	Spray with rotenone or Sevin*[1]; pick by hand and destroy.	Chrysanthemum
Growth tips wilted; small hole in plant stem at point where wilting begins	Borers	Snap off at level of hole; dig out borer and destroy; spray with endosulfan[1], pyrethrum, or rotenone.	Delphinium Iris
Leaves and flowers chewed away; caterpillars on plant	Caterpillars of various kinds and sizes	Pick off by hand and destroy; spray with pyrethrum, malathion[1], or *Bacillus thuringiensis*.	Chrysanthemum Yarrow
Leaves and stems chewed; insects seen hopping and flying	Grasshoppers	Spray with Sevin*[1]; pick off by hand.	Yellow Coneflower
Leaves peppered with small, round holes; small, triangular-shaped bugs seen when disturbed	Leaf Hoppers	Spray with malathion[1] or methoxychlor[1]; dust with diatomaceous earth.	Chrysanthemum Coreopsis
Leaves "painted" with whitish, curling trails	Leaf Miners	Spray with malathion[1]; remove and destroy badly infested leaves.	Columbine Pink

26

INSECTS AND ANIMALS (continued)

SYMPTOM	CAUSE	CURE	PLANTS
Silvery slime trails on plants; soft sticky slugs on plants after dark (check with flashlight)	Slugs and Snails	Set out shallow containers of beer; set out metaldehyde slug bait[1]; pick by hand after dark or on dark days.	Daylily Hosta Phlox
Leaves yellowing with speckled look; fine spider webs on backs of leaves and at point where leaves attach to stem; very tiny bugs on backs of leaves	Spider Mites	Spray with a miticide[1] from underneath to hit backs of leaves; wash or spray with soapy water.	Yellow Coneflower Daylily
Small glob of white bubbles on plant stem or leaves; small insect hidden inside	Spittlebugs	Ignore unless very pervasive; spray with malathion[1]; wash off repeatedly with water from hose.	Chrysanthemum
Brown or white flecks on plant leaves	Thrips	Spray with malathion[1] or dust with sulfur.	Daylily

DISEASES

SYMPTOM	CAUSE	CURE	PLANTS
Leaves become mottled, curl, and shrivel; plants become deformed	Blights and Viruses	Remove and destroy plants; buy blight-resistant strains; do not smoke; wash hands before handling plants.	Japanese Anemone Lupine
Newly sprouted seedlings fall over and die	Damping Off	Start seeds in sterile soil mix. Dust seeds with Captan*[1] before planting.	All plants
Round, dusty brown or black spots on leaves; leaves drop from plant	Leaf Spot	Remove badly diseased leaves and destroy; spray with benomyl[1] or zineb[1].	Chrysanthemum Iris Phlox
Lower leaves and stems turn grayish and look slightly wilted	Powdery Mildew	Increase air circulation; spray with benomyl[1] or sulfur.	Bachelor's Button Delphinium Phlox
Orange or reddish-brown raised dots form on backs of leaves; leaves look wilted	Rust	Increase air circulation; keep foliage dry; buy rust-resistant varieties; spray with ferbam[1] or zineb[1]; spray flowers with sulfur or benomyl.	Snapdragon Hollyhock Yarrow

[1] = Inorganic treatment.
* = Copyrighted brand name.

Preparing for Winter

Mulching perennials protects them from the ravages of winter.

Once early frost hits, you'll find that the top growth will die back on most perennials. When this occurs, use hand pruners to cut off the dead stems, leaving only the bottom 2 to 3 inches. Varieties such as mountain pink and stonecrop, which don't die down, should *not* be cut back.

These cutoff stalks as well as any fallen leaves, flowers, and other garden debris should be removed from the beds and disposed of at this time. Add them to your compost pile if you have one, burn them, or put them into the rubbish bin. This will get rid of any insects or diseases.

Continue deep-watering perennials until the ground has solidly frozen. If plants go into winter in a dry condition, they're likely to suffer badly—even die—from winter sun and winds.

In those sections of the country that are warm, no further winter protection is needed. The same is true of the most northern areas, where a deep snow cover protects plants from sun and wind drying as well as from soil temperature fluctuations. It's in those intermediate zones, where snow cover comes and goes and air temperature changes erratically above and below freezing levels that perennials suffer badly from winter damage. In these areas, a protective layer should be laid over the plants and surrounding soil once the ground becomes frozen hard—the idea here is to keep the soil and plants *cold* throughout the winter.

Use whatever is available to provide this protective layer. Saltmarsh hay (difficult to find nowadays and expensive), pine needles, straw, shredded leaves, or evergreen boughs are all good alternatives. This protection should be removed as soon as the frost has left the ground and the lawn feels squishy underfoot. If you've used evergreen branches, remove and discard them; the other protective alternatives can remain as mulching around the plants, if desired. However, they should be removed from the top and drawn back away from the crowns. Usually the mulch will have settled and decomposed over winter so that only 3 to 4 inches remain. If the mulch layer is deeper than this, take off the excess and store it for later use. Bulbs planted under the mulch will be able to poke up through it.

Not all perennials require winter protection. Many old standbys survive very well without any special winter care. Among these are bearded and Siberian iris, peony, columbine, hosta, phlox, and pink bleeding heart.

Plants standing in water from winter thaws is another problem to avoid. When you set the plants in the ground, be sure that the crowns are at or very slightly above ground level. Then, in the early fall, level out any water-holding dams you may have had around the plants. If these are left in place, you run the risk of losing the plants to rot during the winter. Those most susceptible to this problem include delphiniums, foxgloves, and coralbells. It isn't a good situation for any perennials other than those that enjoy having "wet feet."

As you study the plant descriptions and cultural notes in the directory section, you'll see that a reference to hardiness zones is given for each plant listed. This indicates the coldest winter temperatures that plants can normally be expected to survive without difficulty. Catalogs also list the hardiness zones for plants they're offering; be guided by these.

Naturally, there are temperature variations within a hardiness zone; towns only ten miles apart often experience a temperature difference of ten degrees or more. Different sections of a single garden can vary, too—some parts are sheltered, while cold air always drains or settles in certain areas. Therefore, you need to judge whether *your* local conditions are colder or warmer than the averages given for your zone, and make your selections accordingly. By placing less hardy plants in a spot that is sheltered and faces south, you may be able to grow some varieties that wouldn't otherwise survive in your yard. In general, it's a good idea to select from those that are considered hardy in your own or colder zones.

Cutting Back Stems After Frost

After the first hard frost has killed back the leaves of perennials, use hand pruners to cut the stems back to about 3 inches from the ground. Dispose of the stems and leaves by composting or, if there have been infestations of disease and insects, by burning. Sprinkle a handful of bonemeal around each plant for slow feeding over winter.

Applying a Winter Mulch

Once the ground is frozen hard, a winter mulch layer should be used. Choose a light and loose mulch—one that will allow air and water to pass through easily. Nonmatting leaves such as oak and evergreen boughs (a great recycling use for your Christmas tree!) are two excellent choices. This mulch will keep the ground cold during winter thaws, thus reducing the likelihood of heaving. It will also reduce the possibility of windburn and sunburn when there is no protective snow layer. Remove this winter mulch as soon as frost has left the ground in very early spring.

Protecting Perennials in Winter

Perennials that are marginally hardy in your zone can sometimes be given adequate extra protection to survive. Wood or wire frames covered with burlap can be set over such plants after the protective winter mulch layer has been applied. Polystyrene cones, designed to protect roses over winter, can be used in this same manner.

Shredded Leaves as Mulch

Shredded leaves are an excellent and easy way to obtain mulch. Once shredded, any type of leaves can be used. Shred them with a shredder/chipper, or run your rotary lawn mower over a mound of them several times, blowing the leaves back toward themselves each time. A 6- to 8-inch layer around the plants, with just the growth crown left uncovered, works well. By spring, the bottom layer will have broken down into nourishing humus; any excess mulch can be removed.

Zone Map: When's the Last Frost in Your Area?

The United States Department of Agriculture Plant Hardiness Zone Map is a guide designed to link frost dates with regions. It divides the United States into 10 zones based on average minimum winter temperatures, with Zone 1 being the coldest in North America and Zone 10 the warmest. Each zone is further divided into sections that represent 5-degree differences within the 10-degree zone.

This map should only be used as a general guideline, since the lines of separation between zones are not as clear cut as they appear. Plants recommended for one zone might do well in the southern part of the adjoining colder zone, as well as in the neighboring warmer zone. Factors such as altitude, exposure to wind, and amount of available sunlight also contribute to a plant's winter hardiness. Also note that the indicated temperatures are average minimums—some winters will be colder and others warmer than this figure.

Even though the USDA Plant Hardiness Zone Map is not perfect, it is *the* most useful single guide for determining which plants are likely to survive in your garden and which ones are not.

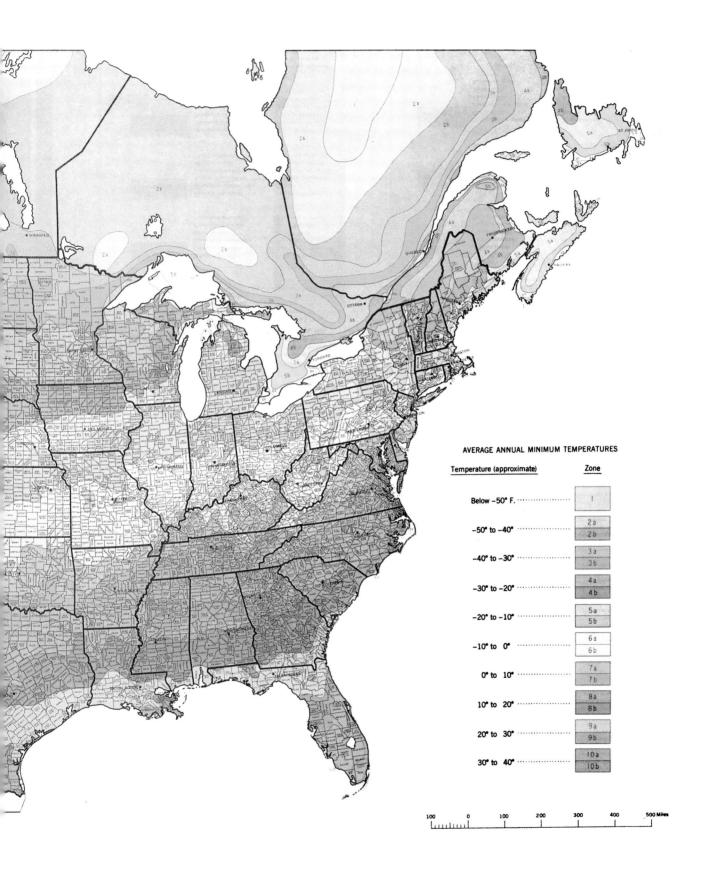

AVERAGE ANNUAL MINIMUM TEMPERATURES

Temperature (approximate)	Zone
Below –50° F.	1
–50° to –40°	2a / 2b
–40° to –30°	3a / 3b
–30° to –20°	4a / 4b
–20° to –10°	5a / 5b
–10° to 0°	6a / 6b
0° to 10°	7a / 7b
10° to 20°	8a / 8b
20° to 30°	9a / 9b
30° to 40°	10a / 10b

100   0   100   200   300   400   500 Miles

The Magic of Propagating New Plants

Starting from Seed

These small perennials are growing very well outdoors.

Perennials can be started from seed indoors during the winter months, or directly in the garden during the growing season. Those started indoors in advance of the growing season will often bloom during their first season in the garden; those started outdoors probably will not.

Outdoor planting can be done almost any time of the year, although in colder climates seeds started in early fall may not develop deep enough roots to survive the winter. Generally, seed starting in spring and early summer is more successful.

Seedbeds should be of a good light loam with moist peat moss or other humus mixed in. They should be located in light shade; if this is not possible, some shading should be provided for the first few weeks after planting. When starting small amounts of seed, a good approach is to sow them in shallow boxes filled with seed starter mix, just as you would if starting them indoors (this sterile soilless mix eliminates the problem of losing young seedlings to disease or to crowding out by weeds), and placing the boxes in a location where they receive plenty of light but little direct sun.

Sprouting plants will first unfold their seed leaves; within these will be the growth bud for producing their true leaves. When the young seedlings reach the stage where they have their first set of true leaves, they're ready to be carefully transplanted to individual clay, plastic, or peat pots. When they become large enough to survive without special care, they're ready to be planted permanently into the garden.

When starting seeds indoors, it's often difficult to provide enough natural light for them to thrive. As a result, they become leggy and weak. It's easy to avoid this problem by installing grow lights over the plants. Grow lights are special fluorescent tubes that provide the full spectrum of light necessary for good plant growth; they're only slightly more expensive than regular fluorescent lights and can be obtained at most garden shops.

Use a regular fluorescent fixture and hang it in a way that will allow you to easily raise and lower it—ideally, it should be kept 6 to 8 inches above the tops of the plants at all times. Seedlings do best with 16 to 18 hours of light each day; the easiest way to consistently provide this is by plugging the grow light fixture into a simple on-off lamp timer. Remember that although you want to extend the day length, plants also require some hours of darkness in each 24-hour cycle.

Perennial seeds sprout and grow best at a temperature of about 70° F. Water them with lukewarm rather than ice cold water—it's less shocking and helps the seeds thrive. Be sure to keep the planting mix moist, but avoid having it continuously soaking wet; young plants can drown just as easily as they can die from drying out. Once the seeds have sprouted and seedlings have several sets of true leaves, care regarding watering can relax; it's from the time of planting and during the time of sprouting that seedlings are most vulnerable to improper watering.

Starting Seeds in Peat Pots

As an alternative to starting seeds directly in an outdoor seedbed, it's possible to start them in peat pots or packs. Plant two or three seeds per individual cube, then thin to the sturdiest one when the seedlings are at the proper stage. Start seedlings this way either indoors or outside.

Hardening Off Seedlings

Potted or boxed seedlings should be hardened off for a week or so before transplanting into the garden. This can be done by carrying them outside and leaving them there for a longer time each day before bringing them in overnight. Start by having them outside only one hour, increase to two hours, then four hours, then six hours, etc. This will wean them away from the indoor, hothouselike growing conditions without setting them back from shock. Once the plants have been hardened off, follow planting instructions for container-grown plants.

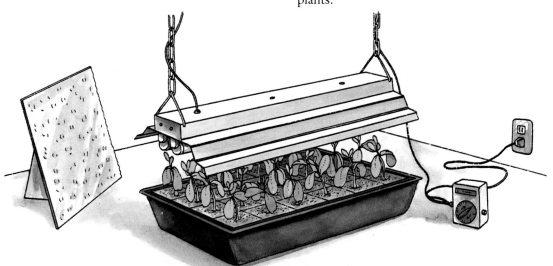

Starting Seeds Under Grow Lamps

Seeds can be started during any season if they are grown indoors under grow lamps. The main requirement is that they receive between 16 and 18 hours of light a day. This is easily managed by plugging grow lights into a lamp timer. Seedlings started in late fall or early winter can easily be grown to a sufficient size for spring planting and blooming.

Starting Stem and Root Cuttings

Chrysanthemums are often started by cuttings.

Many perennials cannot be grown from seed because the plants that result will not be exactly like the parent plant. Instead, these perennials must be propagated asexually—this is known as vegetative reproduction.

One way of doing this is by taking pieces of plant stem or roots and growing them into new plants. Gardeners call these pieces *cuttings*. Not all perennials will generate whole new plants from pieces of themselves, although many do this easily.

Stem Cuttings—Stem cuttings should be taken from the active growing tips of the plant. Cuttings should be between 3 and 6 inches in length, and removed from the parent plant in the evening or in early morning when they're in peak condition. Use only healthy plants that are free from insects and diseases and are in an active growing stage.

Gather cuttings for only five minutes, bringing them indoors to process immediately. This will cut down on the possibility of wilting and the energy loss that accompanies it. After one batch of cuttings has been completed, you can gather additional batches, preparing each and inserting the cuttings into the rooting medium before picking a new group.

Rooting hormone powders, though not absolutely essential, do speed up the rooting process and generally help produce a higher percentage of successful "takes." They're long lasting and inexpensive; the smallest packet is all you'll need for hundreds of cuttings.

A rooting medium must provide good drainage and air circulation. At the same time, it must supply support to the plant stems and enough compaction to keep the stems moist. Coarse sand is the traditional rooting medium, but most growers today use some combination of sand, vermiculite, perlite, and peat moss. A mix of perlite combined with an equal amount of either peat moss or vermiculite provides good drainage and moisture-retention capability.

Always make a hole first before inserting the prepared cutting into the medium. Firm the medium around the stem. Once all the cuttings are inserted, water them to help them settle into the medium, covering them with a plastic bag to form a tent. The cutting leaves should not come in contact with the plastic. If they do, this is a prime environment for rot that will kill the cuttings. To avoid this problem, insert stakes in the medium in such a way that they will hold the plastic away from the cuttings.

Place this tent in a location where the cuttings will receive good light but no direct sun; keep it moist but not wet. The temperature should be about 70° F. Check for roots by gently lifting a cutting from the rooting medium. When roots are ¼-inch long, transplant them into small pots filled with potting mix and grow them until they're sturdy enough to plant outdoors.

Root Cuttings—For just two or three root cuttings, simply dig down beside the parent plant and cut off one or two roots with a knife or hand pruners. For a larger number of root cuttings, dig up the parent plant and trim off all of the side roots. Discard the parent plant, or trim the top back heavily and replant it.

For best results, root cuttings should be taken in early spring (except for oriental poppies, which seem to do better if cuttings are taken in the fall). To help identify the top of the cutting (that part closest to the plant's main root or crown) from the bottom, make cuts straight across the top end and a slanted cut at the bottom end of each segment. Cut fine roots into 1-inch lengths; fleshy ones into 1½- to 2-inch pieces.

Cuttings of fine roots can be scattered horizontally over the surface of the rooting medium (rich sandy loam is best) and covered with about ½ inch of soil or sand. Fleshy roots are planted upright in the medium, 2 to 3 inches apart, with the top ¼ inch of the cutting sticking out of the ground.

Unlike stem cuttings that root within weeks, root cuttings are slow to generate new top growth.

Keep them in a sunny location out of direct sun, and continue to water them whenever the rooting medium begins to dry. Water then with a water-soluble fertilizer once growth appears.

How to Start Perennials from Stem Cuttings

1 Cut 3- to 6-inch growth tips from the parent plant with a small, sharp knife. Make a clean, slanted cut just above a leaf node, side shoot, or growth bud. The parent plant should be in a stage of active growth with young and succulent stems. If the stems are woody and difficult to cut, try recutting closer to the tip. Dip the lower one-third to one-half of the stem in rooting powder; this is a hormone stimulant that helps encourage root growth. Gently tap the stem to knock off excess powder.

2 Poke a hole in the rooting medium and insert a cutting to between one-third and one-half of its length. Firm the rooting medium around the stem with your fingers. When all the cuttings are inserted, water them in place. A large, clear plastic bag forms a mini-greenhouse over the cuttings. Insert sticks or stakes around the container edge to hold the plastic away from the cuttings. Lift the edge of the plastic for an hour or so each day to allow air circulation.

3 Gently lift out a cutting to check for roots. Some plants root more quickly than others: It may take from one week to one month for roots to show. When roots are ¼-inch long, use a spoon or fork as a small trowel for lifting out cuttings. Plant them in small 1½- to 2-inch pots filled with potting mix. Wait and replant them into larger pots or into the garden when a good strong root system has formed.

Dividing Perennials

Perennials—especially those that thrive and spread abundantly—need to be dug up and divided every few years. This provides the opportunity to keep the plant within bounds and to remove older, less vital portions, as well as any diseased sections. A natural by-product of this plant division is additional plants, which can be replanted in other parts of your own yard or shared with other gardeners.

Perennials can be divided by taking pieces away from their outer edges—separating them from the main plant by cutting through the crown with a knife or a sharp-bladed spade. You can also lift the entire plant from the ground and pull or cut it apart.

Some plants divide very easily. They're loosely interwoven and can be separated into chunks simply by pulling them apart with your hands. Others are so tightly held together that it becomes a real challenge to break them up. Fortunately, the tough ones are also very hardy and will survive even if you ultimately have to resort to using a meat cleaver or machete! Japanese irises and lupines fall into this latter category.

The primary concerns here are to keep as many of the roots intact as possible, and to have some roots and some foliage in each division. Trim back excess top foliage to balance the loss of feeder roots that takes place when the plants are dug up and torn apart. Avoid the impulse to get as many separate clumps as possible: Larger clumps will thrive, while small divisions are likely to struggle and grow very slowly.

Everywhere but in the South, the best time to divide most perennials is early spring. All but those that flower in early spring should be divided then. Divide the early-spring bloomers right after they've finished blossoming. In warm climates, fall is a better time to divide all perennials except oriental poppies.

There are a few plants—peonies, irises, and oriental poppies—which, even though they bloom in summer, do better if they're divided after they've finished flowering and have begun to change color.

Always plant the new divisions at the same depth as they were growing before lifting. Firm the soil around each new plant and water well to settle the soil closely around the roots. The addition of enough water-soluble fertilizer to make a weak feeding solution during this watering will help get the new plants off to a good start. If nature doesn't provide adequate water during the first

Dividing perennials provides the gardener with additional plants.

several weeks after division, be sure to water as needed.

When dividing plants that have large fleshy roots such as dahlias and bearded irises, it's sometimes confusing to know how to approach them. Dahlias, for instance, hold together in a sort of fan. All of the growth "eyes" are clustered close together at the center of the fan. Divide them in the spring before replanting. Use a sharp knife and carefully cut the cluster apart, making sure there is at least one "eye" with each subgroup of tubers. Iris clumps also need to be cut apart with a sharp knife. Let the divisions air-dry for a half-hour or so after cutting before replanting them—this will give the wounds some time to seal over, thus cutting down on the possibility of rot or infection.

Division of Perennial Clumps by Hand

The simplest way to divide loosely woven perennial clumps is by pulling them apart with your hands, or by digging off a portion with a trowel or spade. Divide them into several large clumps rather than into many very small ones; this will provide less plants, but they'll be more vital and sure to produce flowers the first season after division.

Using Spading Forks to Divide Perennial Clumps

When the perennial clump is more tightly bound together, two spading forks can be stuck through it back-to-back while it's still in the ground. By pushing out on the fork handles, it's usually possible to pry the clump apart. Some are so tenacious, however, that they must be hacked into chunks with a heavy knife, cleaver, or hatchet. Don't be afraid of doing the plant any harm—those that are this tough won't be fazed by such treatment!

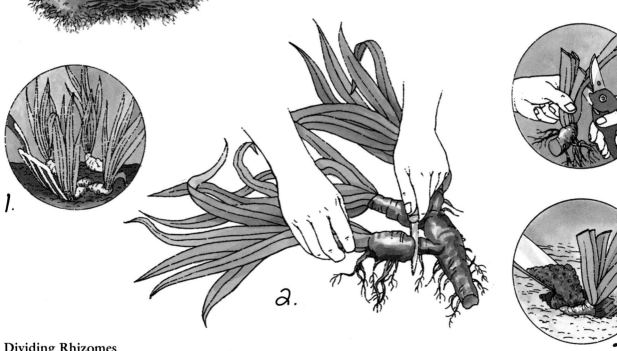

Dividing Rhizomes

Some perennials have large, fleshy underground stems called rhizomes. To divide these types, dig up the entire clump and shake out the dirt. Then use a sharp knife to cleanly cut them into smaller clumps containing three or more buds. Let the pieces air-dry for about an hour so the wounds can seal over before replanting them.

Landscaping with Perennials

Planning a Perennials Garden

This beautiful side border is very eye-catching.

Planning a perennials flower garden for a succession of bloom all season long is a fairly complex undertaking. There are many details to consider, but because they're not demanding, perennials are ideally suited for use as often as possible in borders, entrance gardens, and island beds.

The approach for laying out such plantings is to first consider light and soil preferences, the size and height of plants, the color and form of blooms, foliage texture, and plant growth habit. Then make a list of your plant favorites. Research the characteristics of each plant on the list. Then sketch the layout on a piece of paper and note your choices. For flower beds, lay out detailed plans of exactly which plants will go where. Then take a piece of tracing paper and lay it over the basic plan. Mark those areas where bulbs can be interplanted and choose suitable varieties. Finally, make up "proof sheets," identifying which portions of the garden will be colorful during each segment of the growing season. Check to see whether or not it's well balanced. If not, make switches and changes as necessary. Inevitably, there will be a need for a few changes and substitutions as your garden grows, but by carefully studying your advance plan you can at least avoid the obvious mistakes. From these plans you can then determine how many plants you need of each kind. With this information, you're ready to make your purchases and do your planting.

You do not have to exclusively use perennials in a planting. It's perfectly acceptable, often preferable, to mix annuals with perennials, and even—when the bed space is large enough to allow it—to include trees and evergreens or flowering shrubs in the design.

For example, the unique aspect of an entrance garden is that it will be viewed very briefly. This is an area people are likely to move through quickly rather than linger in or sit and view for an extended period. Therefore, it must be planted simply and for immediate impact. This is not the place for subtle combinations and rare species; it's where a bold, eye-catching display is needed.

This doesn't necessarily mean that it must be bright or garish; repeated or massed groups of white or pastel flowers can be effective, too. Even an all-foliage display can be dramatic when well chosen. Hostas, stonecrops, bergenias, Japanese irises, wormwoods, and many others offer wonderful foliage colors and textures to work with.

Plants with strong perfumes are also more likely to be enjoyed in this situation where more subtle perfumes might go unnoticed. Sometimes these strong perfumes, which can be overpowering adjacent to an outdoor sitting area where they're constantly being inhaled, are ideal for short-term enjoyment.

In contrast to entrance gardens, flower plantings that will be enjoyed at leisure either while sitting among them outdoors or viewing them from inside, may be more low key in their design. They should invite the eye to keep coming back for another look to perhaps discover additional aspects that weren't obvious at first. Here, of course, the plantings will be more interesting if there are contrasts of flowers, foliage textures, and colors.

Island beds—plantings that are centrally placed and viewed from all sides—require a somewhat different design approach than side beds. In order to be effective from every direction, it's necessary to lay them out so that the tallest plants are located in the middle of the bed rather than at the rear. It is therefore necessary to have many more plants of low and intermediate heights in these plantings than tall ones. It will not be a difficult undertaking—there are so many varieties to choose from.

Flower beds come in all sizes and outlines; they can be shaped asymmetrically to fit any corner or contour desired. Squared-off, symmetrical beds have a rather formal appearance; curving, meandering ones are more natural and informal looking. Choose a layout that best suits the surrounding garden, your house style, and your personal preferences.

Corner Beds and Side Borders

Borders come in a wide variety of sizes and shapes. Their outline and plant content depend on the surrounding landscape, the land contours, and your own personal tastes.

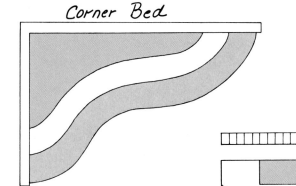

Planning an Island Bed

Island beds are surrounded on all sides by lawn or paving, so they are seen from every direction. It becomes a challenge to have them looking nice from all sides. Planning the layout of an island bed differs from a side border because the tallest flowers are clustered in the center of it, rather than arranged along the back edge.

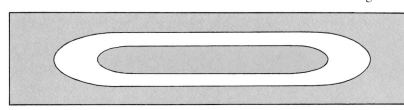

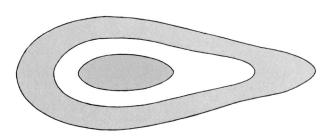

Perennials in Containers

I n most instances, perennials are best grown directly in the ground. However, there are occasions when it's desirable to grow them in containers as potted plants.

When the garden soil is so poor that it's nearly impossible to successfully grow plants in it, container plantings can be the solution. They can also be the answer for soilless locations such as an apartment balcony, a deck, or a patio.

A third reason for raising container-grown perennials is to allow you to have those varieties that are not winter hardy in your climate. By growing them in containers, it's possible to easily move them into the house or a special shelter over the winter, then back into the garden in the spring.

Finally, it's sometimes nice to grow perennials as indoor plants, providing attractive displays within your home. After all, most houseplants are, in fact, perennials that are tropical and therefore not hardy for growing outdoors in most parts of the country. Some gardeners enjoy the novelty of growing various perennial bulbs in containers for winter bloom: Tulips, daffodils, hyacinths, amaryllis, and lilies are popular choices.

Because of the extra care and space year-round container-grown plants require, you'll probably limit yourself to growing only those that are your special favorites—perennials that look beautiful both while they're in bloom and when they are not and those that add appreciably to the decor of your home and garden.

Perennials grow well in containers if they are given proper care.

In order for plants to prosper in containers, a primary rule is that the pots must have adequate water drainage capability. Other major needs of potted plants are frequent watering, regular feeding, and repotting when they show signs of becoming rootbound. An easy way to check is by knocking the plant out of the pot every six months to see how jammed with roots it has become—when they're solidly matted, it's time to shift into a slightly larger pot, or to divide the plant into several pieces and repot.

To carry warm weather plants successfully through the winter in cold climates, it's necessary to bring them into the house or a greenhouse where warmth can be maintained. For those plants that are half-hardy or require only slightly milder winters than those you have, it's possible to place them on an unheated enclosed porch or other similar location where daylight sun can reach them, but they're not subjected to extremely low temperatures. If sub-zero temperatures persist, a small space heater on a low setting will provide enough heat to prevent damage. Don't make it so warm that tender new growth is encouraged to sprout—just fend off the very coldest conditions for the brief periods that they last.

Remember that potted plants overwintered under these conditions will require periodic watering in order to keep them from drying out. Such waterings should be infrequent as the plant's metabolism is much slower in cold conditions.

GOOD PLANT CHOICES TO GROW IN CONTAINERS

Asparagus Fern	Ferns
Rex Begonia*	Geranium
Bleeding Heart	Lavender
Chrysanthemum	Marguerite
Yellow Coneflower	Oxalis*
Daylily	Poinsettia*
Espalier and Tree	Stonecrop
Forms of	
Chrysanthemum,	
Fuchsia, Geranium,	
and Lantana*	

*=Not winter hardy

Gardening in Containers

This cross-section drawing shows the best way to plant in a container. To grow plants successfully in containers, good drainage is essential. Drainage holes need to be covered to keep in soil: Pieces of broken pottery, fine screening, or a coffee filter may be used. If additional drainage is needed, add a layer of small stones, perlite, or coarse sand in the bottom of the container. If the container is located where dripping water would do damage, place a drip tray under the container to catch excess water.

Using Decorative Containers

When using a decorative container that has no drainage holes, place a well-drained pot inside of it and actually grow the plants in this inner pot. Raise the inner pot on a layer of pebbles to keep it above water level. The space between the inner and outer pots can be filled with peat moss to provide insulation that helps stabilize soil temperatures.

How to Care for Container-Grown Plants

Perennials in containers must receive special care over winter in cold climates. Keep them in the house or a greenhouse if they are tropical varieties. Those that withstand freezing can be kept in an unheated area such as an enclosed porch and will only require some heating during prolonged, extreme cold spells. Watering should be cut back severely during this dormant period.

Directory of Perennial Favorites

This lovely perennials planting is very delicate and airy.

Perennials are certainly versatile plants. They can grow in good soil and poor soil; some flourish in full sun, and others are quite content with deep shade. The sizes and shapes nature provides them with are so diverse that any gardener can select perennials to suit his or her garden location and conditions.

The following directory was designed in order to help gardeners in all regions of the United States make the best perennial selections possible. Botanical and common names, descriptions, ease of care, how-to-grow techniques, propagation, uses, and related species and varieties are all dealt with in detail. Color bars identifying zones that each specimen is congenial to are provided. For example, if a perennial is listed under Zone 5, this means that Zone 5 is the coldest zone at which the plant is hardy. Photos are included for each entry.

The adaptability of perennials truly makes them all-purpose plants. Whether you want to design a garden strictly with perennials or add color to an annuals garden in certain seasons, you will find plants here that will work for you. And if you like what you created, you have the satisfaction of knowing that with a little bit of work your garden can flourish year after year.

Anemone, Japanese

Astilbe; Garden Spiraea

Astilbe tacquetii 'Superba'

Anemone species

Zone: USDA 5b

The genus comes from the Greek word for "wind," and many of the plants in this family are called wind flowers. They are listed as *Anemone* X *hybrida*.

Description: The strong-stemmed and showy flowers have 5 or more petallike sepals that enclose numerous golden stamens with compound and very attractive leaves. Mature clumps can reach a height of 5 feet.

Ease of care: Easy

How to grow: These plants are not difficult to grow but do need a fertile, moist soil with plenty of organic matter mixed in as the roots (or rhizomes) resent heavy clay and wet earth and will rot in those conditions. Anemones enjoy full sun in Northern gardens but will easily adjust to partial shade. In Southern gardens, they need partial shade. In areas that have severe winters with little snow cover, plants should be mulched in late fall. In colder areas of the country, many flowers are destroyed by early frosts, so they must be protected.

Propagation: By division in early spring or by root division.

Uses: Anemones are especially beautiful when grown in large clumps.

Related varieties: A number of varieties are found including 'Alba' with white flowers, 'Mont Rose' with deep rose flowers, and 'Queen Charlotte' bearing semi-double, pink flowers. *Anemone vitifolia* is similar, but the pink-blossomed plants are hardier and more tolerant to both sun and drier soil. It is usually sold as 'Robustissima' and blooms a month earlier than *Anemone* X *hybrida*.

Astilbe species

Zone: USDA 5

Beautiful plants for the garden, the astilbes available to gardeners today are usually the result of hybridizing and listed as *Astilbe* X *Arendsii* in garden books and nursery catalogs. The botanical name means "without brilliance" and refers to the lack of punch in the individual flowers.

Description: Astilbes are lovely plants both for their dark green, fernlike foliage growing on polished stems and their long panicles (or spikes) of flowers that resemble feathery plumes. Individual blossoms are small, but as each head contains dozens of branches and each branch bears hundreds of flowers, the total effect is one of beauty. Depending on the type, they can bloom from mid-summer to the end of August.

Ease of care: Easy

How to grow: Astilbes do well in full sun but are best with partial shade, especially in the southern parts of the country. Soil should be good and moist with plenty of organic matter mixed in. Divide the clumps every third year.

Propagation: By division.

Uses: The larger varieties work well in the garden border as specimen plants, even though most of them should be set out in groups of three or more. Colors include white, pink, red, rose, and lilac. Heights vary from 12 to 40 inches. The white forms are especially effective against a shrub border or a line of bushes. They also make an effective ground cover. Astilbes turn a lovely shade of brown in the fall with the dried flower heads persisting until beaten down by heavy snow. They can be used as cut flowers in the summer and then dried for winter floral arrangements. Finally, astilbes can be forced for winter flowering by potting them in the fall, rooting, and bringing them into greenhouse heat with plenty of water.

Related species: *Astilbe chinensis* 'Pumila' originally came from China and Japan. The flowers are a mauve-pink on 8- to 12-inch stems, perfect along the edge of a border and in the rock garden since they can tolerate a drier soil than others. *Astilbe tacquetii* 'Superba' is also from China and bears large plumes of rose-pink flowers resembling cotton candy on 4-foot stems.

Related varieties: 'Bridal Veil' bears white flowers on 2-foot stems; 'Peach Blossom' has salmon-pink flowers on 26-inch stems; pink 'Erica' is on 30-inch stems; and 'Montgomery' is a clear red on 28-inch stems.

Avens

Baby's Breath

Balloon Flower

Geum species

Zone: USDA 6

The avens are members of the rose family. They produce brilliant flowers and plants with attractive leaves coated with silky down. *Geum* is the original Latin name for the herb Bennet *(Geum urbanum)*, a plant with an astringent root once used in medicine. Most of the garden forms are hybrids of two or more species.

Description: Avens are clumps of attractive, lobed, shiny green leaves covered with silky down on hairy stems. The plants grow to 2 feet tall and bear single flowers about 1½ inches across. They bloom in spring and summer.

Ease of care: Easy

How to grow: Avens are plants for cool summers. They prefer full sun and a well-drained but moist soil with plenty of humus. The plants should be divided every two years. In areas subject to below zero temperatures without snow cover, these plants should be mulched.

Propagation: By division in spring or by seed.

Uses: Avens are attractive in the front of a border and in a rock garden where the bright flowers are very showy.

Related varieties: 'Mrs. Bradshaw' is a double, brilliant scarlet and 'Lady Stratheden' is a warm yellow.

Gypsophila paniculata

Zone: USDA 5

Almost everyone has given or received a bouquet of flowers from the florist that contained a few sprays of baby's breath. The genus is Latin for the phrase "friendship with gypsum," because one species, *Gypsophila repens,* has been found growing on gypsum rocks.

Description: Small, blue-green leaves, almost fleshy, on stems with slightly swollen joints bear a profusion of many-branched panicles containing numerous ⅛-inch wide flowers. Plants bloom in June and July.

Ease of care: Easy

How to grow: Baby's breath require full sun and a good, deep, well-drained garden soil with humus. Even though the plants have tap roots, they still require liberal amounts of water. If the soil is at all acid, a cup of ground limestone per square yard should be added into the soil surrounding these lime-loving plants. Tall plants will probably require staking. They will rebloom if spent flowers are removed.

Propagation: By seed. Propagation by cuttings requires patience, skill, and luck.

Uses: Baby's breath are wonderful for filling in gaps in a bed or border. They are especially lovely when tumbling over rock walls or falling out of a raised bed.

Related species: *Gypsophila repens* is a creeping baby's breath that grows only 6 inches high, but covers an area to a width of 3 feet. 'Alba' is white; 'Rosea' is pink.

Related varieties: Two popular varieties are 'Bristol Fairy,' with pure white, double flowers that grows to a height of 4 feet and 'Pink Fairy,' reaching 18 inches in height with pink doubles.

Platycodon grandiflorus

Zone: USDA 4

A one-species genus, balloon flowers are so named because the unopened flowers look like small and rounded hot-air blimps. They are originally from Japan. The *genus* is named for the Greek word for "broad bell" and refers to the flower shape.

Description: Balloon flowers are clump-forming perennials with alternate leaves of a light green on stems usually between 1½ and 3 feet tall. They bear balloon-shaped buds that open to bell-shaped flowers with 5 points and are 2 to 3 inches wide. The sap is milky.

Ease of care: Easy

How to grow: Balloon flowers like moist, well-drained soil in full sun or partial shade. They prefer places with cool summers. Plan the plant's position carefully as it is not until late spring that the first signs of life appear.

Propagation: By division in mid-spring or by seed.

Uses: Blooming for most of the summer, balloon flowers are attractive in borders, with the smaller types growing best along garden edges. They are especially effective when used in conjunction with white pansies or white obedient plants.

Related varieties: 'Album' bears white flowers and 'Hakona Blue' has two layers of petals, both on 16-inch stems. 'Mariesii' has blue flowers on 12- to 16-inch stems and 'Shell Pink' bears larger flowers of a soft-pink on 2-foot stems and is best in some shade.

Basket-of-Gold, Goldentuft, Madwort, Gold-Dust

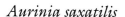

Aurinia saxatilis

Zone: USDA 5

Originally included in the *Alyssum* genus, these charming spring flowers have now been moved to an older genus named after a chemical dyestuff used to stain paper. They belong to the mustard family.

Description: Attractive and low gray foliage growing in dense mats gives rise to clusters of golden-yellow, 4-petaled flowers floating 6 to 12 inches above the plants.

Ease of care: Easy

How to grow: Aurinias need only well-drained, average soil in full sun. Plants will rot in damp locations and resent high humidity. They can be sheared back after blooming.

Propagation: By cuttings or by seed.

Uses: Aurinias are quite happy growing in the spaces between stone walks, carpeting the rock garden, or growing in pockets in stone walls where their flowers become tumbling falls of gold.

Related varieties: *Alyssum montanum,* 'Mountain Gold,' 4 inches tall, with silvery, evergreen leaves and fragrant, bright yellow flowers makes a dense ground cover. 'Citrina' bears lemon-yellow flowers; 'Flore Plena' has double, yellow blooms; and 'Compacta' has a denser habit of growth.

Bellflower

Campanula species

Zone: USDA 4

The botanical name is from the Latin word for "bell" and refers to the shape of the flowers. The genus includes annual flowers, biennials, and perennials suitable for the formal garden and the wild garden. *Campanula rapunculoides* is a wild weed and should be avoided. *C. rapunculus* can be considered for the vegetable garden, since the rampion has roots that are used in salads.

Description: Bellflowers are usually various shades of blue, and many are available in white. Flowers bloom from late spring into early summer. Basal leaves are usually broader than the stem leaves and form rosettes or mats.

Ease of care: Easy

How to grow: Bellflowers need a good, moist but well-drained soil with plenty of organic matter mixed in. In the North, plants will tolerate full sun as long as the soil is not dry, but elsewhere a spot in semi-shade is preferred.

Propagation: By division or by seed.

Uses: According to the species, plants are beautiful in the border, useful in the rock garden, and fine for the shade or wild garden. Many species, including *Campanula isophylla,* the star of Bethlehem, also do well when grown in pots.

Related species: *Campanula carpatica* is from the Carpathian mountains of Europe, blooming at a height of 10 inches with solitary blue flowers. It is effective as an edging or tumbling over a small rock cliff. Among the many varieties: A white form called 'Alba' as well as 'Blue Carpet,' a smaller,

Campanula glomerata 'Joan Eliot'

more compact form. *Campanula Elatines var garganica,* originally from the Mount Gargano region of Italy, is a plant best set in partial shade where it will flower at a height of 6 inches with bright blue, star-shaped flowers. *Campanula glomerata,* or the clustered bellflower, usually bears a dozen blossoms in tight clusters at the top of a 14-inch stem. 'Crown of Snow' bears large, white flowers. *Campanula persicifolia,* or peach bells, bear flowers on stems up to 3 feet high and prefer moist soil. They are most effective when naturalized at the edge of a wood or shrub border. Flowers are either white or of various shades of blue. 'Grandiflora Alba' bears large, white flowers; 'Blue Gardenia' has deep silvery blue blossoms; and 'Telham Beauty' has larger, china-blue flowers. *Campanula poscharskyana* is a ground creeper with star-shaped, 1-inch blossoms of lavender-blue, perfect for the rock garden or in a hanging basket. *Campanula rapunculoides,* or the creeping bellflower, is a weed from Eurasia that is now naturalized along roadsides from Canada south to Delaware, then west to Illinois. *Campanula rapunculus* is native to the fields of Italy. Its fleshy roots were once cultivated as a salad crop. It bears small blue flowers in long chains that bloom over a long period.

Bergamot, Bee-Balm, Oswego-Tea

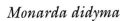

Monarda didyma

Zone: USDA 4

These are stunning, native American plants that have been garden favorites for decades. They are closely related to culinary mint and all have aromatic foliage. Bergamots get their name from Nicolas Monardes.

Description: Sturdy, square stems growing to 4 feet tall have simple leaves. They are topped by crowns that are studded with lipped, usually bright red flowers blooming from summer into fall.

Ease of care: Easy

How to grow: At ease in almost any soil, bergamots prefer a slightly moist spot and full sun, becoming somewhat floppy when grown in the shade. Extra water during dry periods is appreciated. The plants are spreaders, so excess plants should be removed from time to time. Spent flowers should also be removed for extended bloom. Clumps must be divided every few years to keep them healthy.

Propagation: By seed or by division in early spring.

Uses: Useful for the wild garden in moist soil or by the waterside, they are also beautiful in beds or borders because of their long season of bright bloom. Flowers are beloved by hummingbirds and butterflies.

Related varieties: 'Blue Stocking' is not really blue, but a brilliant, deep violet and 'Mahogany' is a deep wine red. Both are on 36-inch stems. 'Cambridge Scarlet' is an old type with brilliant, scarlet flowers; 'Croftway Pink' is a clear rose-pink; and 'Snow White' is white—all are on 30-inch stems.

Bergenia, Heartleaf

Bergenia cordifolia

Zone: USDA 4

Bergenias are plants from Siberia and Mongolia. As such they are perfectly happy in low temperatures when covered with snow. They are named in honor of Karl August von Bergen, a German physician and botanist.

Description: Thick, rounded, evergreen leaves, often 1 foot long, grow from a single crown and are edged with red in cold weather. Flowers are pink with waxy petals, blooming in drooping clusters.

Ease of care: Easy

How to grow: These plants prefer light shade and, without snow cover, protection from bitter winds. They also need good, moist soil with plenty of organic matter.

Propagation: By division or by seed.

Uses: Excellent as an edging in the border or planted in groups on slopes, bergenias are also a fine addition to the rock garden. The leaves are often used in floral arrangements and will last a month in water.

Related species: The winter bergenia, *Bergenia ciliata,* hails from West Pakistan and has large, rounded leaves that are densely hairy on both sides. *Bergenia purpurescens* (often called *B. delavayi*) has dark green leaves that turn a beetroot-red in winter.

Related varieties: The bergenias have been hybridized over many years, leaving parentage often confused. Among the varieties available are 'Evening Bells' with bright red winter foliage and rose-pink flowers; 'Evening Glow' with maroon-cored leaves in winter and flowers of a magenta-crimson said to be hardier than most; and 'Silverlight,' bearing blush-white flowers.

Blanket Flower

Gaillardia x grandiflora

Zone: USDA 4

Cheerful and bright daisylike flowers, *gaillardias* are named in honor of Gaillard de Clarentonneau, a French botanist.

Description: This particular species is a hybrid of two others, more vigorous than the native types and often blooming the first year from seed. Slightly hairy leaves are usually basal; 3- to 4-inch flowers have purple centers (disk flowers) and notched petals (ray flowers) in a number of bright colors. They bloom throughout summer.

Ease of care: Easy

How to grow: Blanket flowers need full sun and a good, but not too fertile, well-drained garden soil. Sometimes short-lived, the plants will not survive a winter in wet soil. Each year, the center of the crown dies back and new plants appear off center. They are easily transplanted to bloom that summer. They bloom over a long period even if spent blossoms are not removed.

Propagation: By division in early spring or by seed.

Uses: *Gaillardias* are suited for the front of a border, particularly if grouped in threes or fives. They also provide marvelous cut flowers. The dwarf varieties are fine as edging plants.

Related varieties: There are a number of varieties available with new types showing up every year. The 'Monarch Strain' has a good choice of reds, yellows, and browns, and 'Goblin' is a dwarf reaching a 12-inch height and bearing red flowers with yellow borders.

Bleeding Heart

Bugleweed

Bugloss, Siberian

Dicentra species

Zone: USDA 4

These heart-shaped pendant flowers with spurs at the base (the genus name means "two-spurred") have attractive foliage until mid-summer.

Description: Bleeding hearts have clusters of rose, pink, or white flowers on arching sprays and bluish, fernlike foliage. Roots are fleshy and sold by the number of eyes present on plant starts.

Ease of care: Easy

How to grow: Bleeding hearts need open or partial shade with an evenly moist soil on the acid side containing plenty of humus. Plenty of peat moss must be used when planting; mulching is done with pine needles or pine bark.

Propagation: By division in early spring or by seed.

Uses: This plant is a lovely sight when planted next to a moss-covered log with ferns in the background or between the gnarled roots of a large tree.

Related species: *Dicentra eximia,* or the fringed bleeding heart flowers, do best in late spring, but if protected from hot sun and given plenty of moisture, they will bloom until frost. Their height is 18 inches. 'Alba' has white flowers. *Dicentra formosa* is a rose-colored species found from British Columbia to California. It is usually about 18 inches high. *Dicentra spectabilis* is the old garden favorite from Japan with deep pink flowers blooming from May to June on 24-inch stems. Except in rare instances, this plant will go dormant by mid-summer, so it is best screened.

Related variety: *Dicentra* X 'Luxuriant' is a hybrid that will bloom throughout the summer, especially if old flowers are removed.

Ajuga species

Zone: USDA 3b

Bugleweeds are excellent both for the color of the leaves and the attractive flowers. The botanical name refers to the shape of the leaves that cover the flower.

Description: Flat, rounded leaves form mats that can keep weeds from making headway. They bloom in May and June with irregular flowers in spiked clusters.

Ease of care: Easy

How to grow: Bugleweeds are easy to grow in ordinary, well-drained garden soil, with full sun or partial shade. As a ground cover, plants should be placed 10 inches apart; they will soon fill in. In areas with mild winters or under good snow cover, they are evergreen.

Propagation: By division in spring or fall.

Uses: Bugleweeds are excellent as ground cover and are also beautiful when used as edgings at the front of a border. In a rock garden, they are perfect for tumbling over rock edges. Although they grow quickly, plants are easily uprooted.

Related species: Two species are generally available: *Ajuga pyramidalis* bears brilliant blue flowers on 6-inch spikes, hovering above deep green leaves, and stays bushy, not spreading as widely as others in the clan. In the fall, the leaves turn to purple-bronze. *Ajuga reptans* is the ground cover of note.

Related varieties: 'Metallica Crispa' has purplish-brown leaves with crisped edges and 'Alba' bears white flowers. 'Burgundy Glow' bears blue flowers with leaves in three colors: New growth is burgundy-red, but as the leaves age, they become creamy white and then dark pink. 'Rosea' has rose flowers.

Brunnera macrophylla

Zone: USDA 4

From western Siberia, these plants are perennial forget-me-nots, named in honor of Swiss botanist Samuel Brunner. Some catalogs still call it *Anchusa myosotidiflora.*

Description: Showy blue flowers about ¼ inch across bloom in clusters during spring. The leaves are large and heart-shaped on slightly hairy stems. Plants can reach 2 feet in height but usually remain at 18 inches.

Ease of care: Easy

How to grow: Brunneras prefer a deep, moist soil with plenty of organic matter in full sun (only in the North) or partial shade. They will, however, do reasonably well in a dry spot if they have shade.

Propagation: By division or by seed.

Uses: They are lovely in the front of a border but are exceptionally attractive when naturalized at the border of a wooded area or in a wild garden along a stream or by a pool. After blooming, the large leaves make an effective ground cover.

Candytuft

Chrysanthemum

Chrysanthemum Superbum 'Wirral Supreme'

Iberis sempervirens
Zone: USDA 4

Many species of candytuft originally came from Iberia, the ancient name of Spain. Hence the genus of *Iberis*. They bloom in the spring.

Description: Candytuft is a many-branched, small, evergreen shrub with smooth, oblong leaves about 1½ inches long. In the spring, it bears flat-topped clusters of white flowers, sometimes flushed with pink. Height can reach 10 inches, spreading to about 20 inches.

Ease of care: Easy

How to grow: Candytufts need good, well-drained garden soil in a sunny spot. They are usually evergreen, but in most areas of Zone 4, winter results in severe damage to the leaves. Mulching is necessary if snow is lacking. Dead branches need to be cut off for growth to begin again. Pruning back after spring flowering is recommended.

Propagation: By division or by seed.

Uses: Candytufts are great for a rock garden where they can tumble about and over rocks. They are also excellent as edging in a border and are suited for growing in pots.

Related varieties: 'Autumn Snow' stays about 10 inches high and blooms twice—in spring and in fall. 'Little Gem' is a dwarf at a 6-inch height.

Chrysanthemum species
Zone: USDA 4 to 6

Chrysanthemums are members of the daisy clan, numbering over 200 species of ornamental plants. One member of the species is the source of the insecticide pyrethrum; another is eaten in the Orient in salads. The genus is Greek for "golden flower."

Description: Leaves are usually divided, often aromatic, and sometimes in basal rosettes. Stems are strong and flowers are showy—either with yellow centers (tubular flowers) surrounded by a row of petals (ray flowers) or a flower head entirely covered with petals as in the florist's mum.

Ease of care: Easy to moderately difficult

How to grow: As a class of plants, chrysanthemums want good, well-drained soil in full sun. Most have shallow roots, so the soil should be evenly moist with frequent applications of fertilizer. The majority of chrysanthemums are late-blooming, short-day plants with flowers initiated by decreasing day length. They benefit from frequent pinching, which promotes bushy growth. Without adequate snow cover, these plants benefit from mulching in the North.

Propagation: By cuttings, by division, or by seed.

Uses: Garden mums (*Chrysanthemum X morifolium*) come in a number of styles including incurved, where petals form a perfect globe; single-flowered, with five or less rows of petals around a central disk; and pompons, with small, button-shaped blossoms. Football and spider mums are always popular. Blue is the only color not available. Seeds sown in early spring will flower around October.

Mums can be purchased as rooted cuttings from nursery suppliers to be set out after all frost danger has passed. They are pinched back for bushy growth and bloom in the late summer and fall. In the fall, potted mums can also be purchased from garden centers and transplanted around the garden where they will continue to bloom until severe frost cuts them down. They also do well in containers.

Related species: *Chrysanthemum coccineum,* or the painted daisy, is a minor source of pyrethrum and a major source of cut flowers. Leaves are fernlike and blossoms come in a number of shades of red, pink, and white on 30-inch stems, blooming in June. They must be cut back to the ground after blooming for a second crop of flowers. *Chrysanthemum X superbum,* or the shasta daisy, produces 4-inch flowers on 1- to 3-foot stems. They prefer cool summers and need some shade in the South. Spotted throughout the border, they bloom from summer to fall and make excellent cut flowers. 'Miss Muffet' has white flowers in early summer; 'Aglaya' is a double, white flower on 26-inch stems blooming from June to September; and 'Cobham Gold' has large, double, cream-colored flowers blooming in summer. *Chrysanthemum nipponicum,* or the Nippon daisy, bears white flowers on 2-foot woody stems, which bear thick, scalloped leaves. They resemble small bushes. These plants cannot be divided, but new plants do grow about the base. Early frost will ruin the flowers, so care must be taken to cover them. The foliage is very aromatic. Nippon daisies are excellent in seaside gardens.

Chrysanthemum coccineum 'Red Dwarf'

Columbine

Aquilegia vulgaris 'Munstead'

Chrysanthemum pacificum is a new plant on the nursery scene. It forms a dense, low-growing ground cover with suc-culentlike foliage. Its leaves have distinct silver-green margins; plants grow 4 to 6 inches high. Clusters of golden-yellow flow-ers resembling the common tansy appear in October but are often cut down by frost in the North. Runners of one plant are said to cover a 3 × 4-foot area in three years. *Chrysanthemum Parthenium,* or feverfew, is still called *Matricaria* in some catalogs. It is an old medical herb, the common name referring to the plant's use as an aid in reducing fever and curing headaches. Bushy plants grow to 3 feet with aromatic leaves. 'Double White' bears double, white flowers on 2-foot stems and 'Aureum' bears little, white flowers on leaves of a golden-yellow color. *Chrysanthemum Weyrichii* is a fairly recent Japanese import that flowers in very late fall with 2-inch single flowers with a yellow eye. 'Pink Bomb' bears flowers with soft, pink petals on 12-inch stems. 'White Bomb' has white flowers in great profusion. *Chrysanthemum Zawadskii,* or the Korean chrysanthemum, is often called *C. rubellum* and is usually available only as 'Clara Curtis.' This plant bears clear pink, single-flowered blossoms that are very hardy.

Aquilegia species
Zone: USDA 4

Columbines are beloved by humming-birds, are perfect for cut flowers, and have a long season of bloom. The genus is from the Latin word for "eagle," probably refer-ring to the spurred petals of the flowers.

Description: The leaves are compound with rounded lobes and are susceptible to insects called leaf miners that tunnel about and produce tracings that often resemble nonsense writing. They do not harm the plants. Flower seasons can be extended by removing all of the spent blossoms before plants go to seed.

Ease of care: Easy

How to grow: Columbines are easy to grow, adapting to almost any reasonably fertile garden soil, although the thick, black roots must have good drainage. They will do well in full sun or partial shade, especially in the South.

Propagation: By propagation in early spring or by seed.

Uses: Since the flowers are both attractive and will bloom over a long period, columbines are excellent in beds and bor-ders. An entire garden could be composed of these blossoms. Flower season can be extended by removing all of the spent blos-soms before plants go to seed.

Related species: *Aquilegia caerulea* is the Colorado columbine with sky-blue blos-soms with white centers on wiry stems growing to 2 feet. *Aquilegia canadensis* is the wild Eastern columbine with graceful flowers having long, red spurs and yellow faces on 1- to 2-foot stems. It is one of the easiest wildflowers to cultivate. Plants want partial shade and well-drained, but not-too-rich, soil. The foliage lasts all year and is often evergreen in milder climates. Perfect in a rock garden, these plants will often seed about in the thinnest layers of soil. They bloom in spring. *Aquilegia chrysantha* is another American native from the South-west that bears yellow flowers on plants up to 3 feet high and blooms over a long sea-son. There is a 1-foot dwarf called 'Nana.' *Aquilegia flabellata* come from Japan and are excellent in the rock garden or as an edging for a border, since the plants are usually 14 inches high or smaller. 'Nana Alba' has pure white flowers on plants under 1 foot high that come from seed.

Related varieties: The hybrid plants vary between 1 to 3 feet in height and are avail-able in many varieties and in many colors. Among the best are the McKana hybrids with 2-foot plants bearing blossoms of blue, pink, maroon, purple, red, and white, and the Music hybrids with 20-inch plants with flowers of intense yellow, blue and white, red and white, and pure white. 'Nora Barlow' has fully double flowers in combi-nations of red, pink, and green. 'Dragonfly' has flowers with longer than average spurs.

49

Coneflower, Purple

Coneflower, Yellow; Black-Eyed Susan

Coralbell, Alumroot

Echinacea purpurea

Zone: USDA 5

This lovely American native was once found naturally from Ohio to Iowa and south to Louisiana and Georgia. The genus is named in honor of the hedgehog because the receptacle (the part that holds the flower proper) is prickly.

Description: Cone-shaped, prickly heads of a bronze-brown are surrounded by rose-purple petals (really ray flowers) on stout stalks from 2 to 4 feet high. Leaves are alternate, simple, and coarse to the touch.

Ease of care: Easy

How to grow: Coneflowers will take almost any well-drained garden soil in full sun. If soil is too good, the flowers must often be staked. Spent flowers should be removed to prolong blooming.

Propagation: By division in spring or by seed.

Uses: Coneflowers are beautiful plants for the back of a small garden border and they are a welcome addition to a wildflower garden. They are especially fine when mixed with gloriosa daisies (*Rudbeckia* spp.) and many of the ornamental grasses. They make excellent cut flowers.

Related species: *Echinacea pallida* is a similar wildflower species from the Midwest with thinner and more graceful petals.

Related varieties: 'White Lustre' and 'White Swan' are two varieties with white flowers; 'Bright Star' bears maroon flowers, and 'Magnus' has rosy purple petals with a dark disk.

Rudbeckia fulgida

Zone: USDA 5

All the members of the genus are native American wildflowers, known collectively as coneflowers. The genus is named in honor of Olaf Rudbeck and his son, both professors of botany.

Description: Coneflowers have hairy, 2- to 3-foot stems with simple, saw-toothed edges. They bear daisies with yellow ray flowers, slightly orange at the base, and purple-brown disk flowers, blooming in July and on to frost.

Ease of care: Easy

How to grow: Although best with a good, moist soil, yellow coneflowers will adapt to any good garden soil that is not too dry or too wet, in full sun. Divide plants every three years.

Propagation: By division or by seed.

Uses: Great flowers for the wild garden or for naturalizing in the meadow garden, 'Goldsturm' is best for the formal bed or border and should be planted in drifts. These flowers are perfect when used in combination with variegated ornamental grasses. They are also excellent for cutting.

Related species: *Rudbeckia laciniata,* or the green-headed coneflower, is valuable for a wild garden. 'Goldquelle' or, as it's sometimes called, 'Gold Drop,' has big, double flowers on 24- to 30-inch stems.

Related varieties: 'Goldsturm' is the plant usually offered by nurseries. About 24 inches high, the golden-yellow flowers bloom profusely in July and August. 'Golden Glow' is found in old-fashioned gardens with its moplike golden heads on 6-foot stems.

Heuchera sanguinea

Zone: USDA 4

Coralbells are American wildflowers originally from New Mexico and Arizona and south to Mexico.

Description: Coralbells are mounds of basal leaves that are rounded and lobed, rising from a thick rootstock. The flowers are tiny bells on 1- to 2-foot slender stems blooming from spring into summer.

Ease of care: Easy

How to grow: In areas of hot summers, these plants like a bit of shade, but usually they prefer as much sun as possible. They should be planted in good, well-drained garden soil with a high humus content and kept somewhat moist. In winter, coralbells resent wet soil and often will die. Every three years they must be divided to prevent crowding. Spent flowers should be removed.

Propagation: By division in spring or by seed.

Uses: Coralbells are lovely in a border or when planted among rocks, rock walls, and in the rock garden. They are also good cut flowers.

Related varieties: 'Bressingham Hybrids' produce flowers in shades of pink to deep crimson and white on 20- to 24-inch stems; 'Chatterbox' has rich, rose-pink flowers on 18-inch stems; 'French White' are white; and 'Pluie de Feu' (or rain of fire) bears cherry-red flowers. 'Purple Palace' has deep mahogany-purple foliage with pale pink flowers.

Coreopsis

Crane's-Bill

Daisy, Michaelmas

Coreopsis species

Zone: USDA 5

Coreopsis is a Greek word for "buglike," referring to the shape of this plant's seeds that were thought to look like ticks. The comparison is not particularly apt.

Description: Small daisies in various shades of yellow and orange on wiry stems up to 3 feet high. Leaves vary from simple, oval shapes in basal rosettes to foliage that is decidedly fernlike.

Ease of care: Easy

How to grow: *Coreopsis* are happy in almost any well-drained garden soil in full sun. They are drought-resistant and an outstanding choice for hot, difficult places.

Propagation: By division in spring or by seed.

Uses: Excellent for the wild garden and in the formal border, these flowers are also prized for cutting. The smaller types are also good for edging plants. *Coreopsis* are suited for patio containers and in hanging baskets. Tying up is often indicated.

Related species: *Coreopsis grandiflora* and *C. lanceolata* are freely interchanged. *Coreopsis auriculata* 'Nana' is a dwarf form that stays about 1 foot tall and bears orange flowers. *Coreopsis grandiflora* 'Sunray' bears double, golden-yellow flowers on 2-foot stems. *Coreopsis lanceolata* 'Goldfink' has golden-yellow flowers on 9-inch stems. 'Brown Eyes' has a ring of dark brown close to the center of golden flowers on 20-inch stems. *Coreopsis verticillata* bears bright yellow flowers on 2-foot mounds of foliage. 'Moonbeam' is a light-cream yellow; 'Golden Showers' bears dozens of yellow flowers on 24- to 30-inch stems; and 'Zagreb' is a long-blooming type with yellow flowers on 18-inch stems.

Geranium species

Zone: USDA 5

Crane's-bill is the common name for this plant because the female part of the flower resembles the shape of a crane's beak. *Geranium* is the genus and is Greek for the same similarity. These plants are not to be confused with the common summer or florist's geranium that is really a *Pelargonium* and at home in South Africa.

Description: Usually low-growing plants with lobed or deeply cut leaves on forked stems bear 5-petaled flowers in great profusion blooming from spring to summer.

Ease of care: Easy

How to grow: Garden geraniums need good, well-drained garden soil in full sun or light shade in areas of hot summers. The larger types will sometimes need staking.

Propagation: By division or by seed.

Uses: In a border or a rock garden, crane's-bills are lovely plants. They make excellent ground cover and are striking when grown along a wall, letting the stems and flowers tumble over the edge. In many of the species, leaves turn red in the autumn.

Related species: *Geranium cinereum* is a low-growing plant usually reaching about 8 inches in height with pink flowers 1 inch across. 'Ballerina' is deep pink and 'Splendens' is a vivid crimson. *Geranium dalmaticum* grows 6 inches high with rose-colored flowers. *Geranium himalayense* (sometimes called *G. grandiflorum*) produces 2-inch wide, violet-blue flowers on 15-inch stems. 'Johnson's Blue' has bright, blue-violet flowers that bloom with dozens of blossoms in June and July. *Geranium sanguineum* reaches 1½ feet in height with violet-red flowers that bloom most of the summer.

Aster species

Zone: USDA 5

The genus name of the asters is the Greek word for "star" and if ever a group of plants deserved such a bright appellation, this is the one.

Description: Daisylike flowers, usually about 1 inch wide with yellow centers are carried on stiff, branched stems with long, narrow leaves. Bushy plants vary from 6 inches to 6 feet high, blooming from late summer into fall. The yellow centers are actually disk flowers and the petals are really ray flowers.

Ease of care: Easy

How to grow: These plants do not need pampering other than good drainage and full sun. They want reasonable garden soil, preferring one that is slightly acid. Although asters in the field can take a great deal of dryness, those in the garden will need water in periods of drought. Plants should be divided every two years since the center of the clumps begins to look tattered. Plants can be pinched to produce neater clumps of flowers or be left alone. Sometimes the taller types require staking.

Propagation: By division in spring. Seedlings of many species can be variable both in growth habit and bloom, but adventurous gardeners might enjoy the challenge.

Uses: The English took the American New York field aster, *Aster novi-belgii,* and the New England aster, *A. novae-angliae,* and produced the Michaelmas daisy through hybridizing. Today the resulting varieties are stalwarts of the late summer and fall garden. The smaller types can be used as edgings for borders; the middle-sized asters are beautiful when grouped according to color; and the largest asters become effective backdrops to other plants.

Daisy (continued)

Daylily

Hemerocallis species

Zone: USDA 4

Asters mix well with ornamental grasses—also blooming in the fall—and late-blooming perennial sunflowers (*Helianthus* species) and sneezeweeds (*Helenium* species).

Related species: The alpine aster, *Aster alpinus,* is a dwarf species with gray-green leaves and yellow-centered, purple-blue flowers, from 1 to 1½ inches wide. They are excellent in the rock garden or in the front of a border, blooming in summer. There are a number of colored forms available. The wild asters, *Aster novae-angliae* and *A. novi-belgii,* the parents of the Michaelmas daisies, are usually too rangy for the formal garden, although variations do occur in the wild that deserve some attention. They are also excellent for the wild garden. The Siberian aster, *Aster tartaricus,* is hardy to USDA Zone 3 and produces light blue flowers on very tall plants, sometimes reaching 7 feet.

Related varieties: From the original *Aster novae-angliae* line come, among others, 'Alma Potschke,' 3 feet tall and bearing deep pink flowers that bloom for almost six weeks; 'September Ruby,' with deep crimson flowers on 40-inch stems; and 'Harrington's Pink,' featuring pure pink flowers on 4-foot stems. For shorter plants look for the *Aster novae-belgii* varieties: 'Alert,' with red flowers on 15-inch plants; 'Pink Bouquet,' with pink flowers on 14-inch plants; and 'Snow Flurry' for white flowers on 15-inch plants.

The scientific name of the wild daylily is *Hemerocallis fulva*—*hemero* being Greek for "beautiful" and *callis* Greek for "day," since each individual blossom opens, matures, and withers in 24 hours or less. *Fulva* is the Latin word for "tawny."

Daylilies first reached England in 1575: Originally they were brought over the trade routes from China. Settlers in America from Europe and England brought these hardy plants to brighten their colonial gardens. Almost every home had tawny daylilies and a clump of lemon lilies, *Hemerocallis Lilio-asphodelus* (once known as *H. flava*). Today there are well over 30,000 varieties with more on the way every year.

Description: Tuberous and fleshy roots with mostly basal, sword-shaped leaves usually grow up to 2 feet long with tall, multi-branched stalks, each containing many 6-petaled lilylike flowers. Once blooming only in summer, new varieties now begin to bloom in May and on into September and include some rebloomers.

Ease of care: Easy

How to grow: Daylilies are literally carefree, wanting only good, well-drained garden soil in full sun. They benefit from partial shade in the South.

Propagation: By division in spring or fall. The species is also propagated by seed.

Uses: Entire gardens can be created using these marvelous plants—dwarf types for rock gardens, species for beds and borders, and varieties for edging. By mixing types, bloom can be present from late spring to fall. The common tawny daylily can be used to hold dry, rocky banks together and for plantings in meadows or wild gardens. The lemon lily is indeed a valuable garden plant.

Flower sizes vary from 3 to over 6 inches, with as many as 30 to 80 flowers on a stem or scape.

Related species: *Hemerocallis citrina* blooms in summer with arching 3½-foot leaves and fragrant, yellow blossoms on 4-foot stems that open in the early evening and last to the following day. *Hemerocallis fulva* is the tawny daylily, too rough for today's perennial bed or border, but still excellent for a ground cover or for a meadow garden. *Hemerocallis lilio-asphodelus* is the old-fashioned lemon lily with fragrant blossoms for late May and June. *Hemerocallis minor* is a dwarf species with yellow, fragrant flowers and grasslike leaves reaching a height of 18 inches.

Related varieties: There are hundreds of daylily varieties available every year from nurseries. The following are noteworthy: *Hemerocallis* 'Bertie Ferris' has midseason blossoms of deeply ruffled persimmon on 15-inch stems; 'Catherine Woodbery' with flowers of a pale, orchid-pink blooming in July on 30-inch stems; 'Chicago Fire,' a brilliant red hybrid with 6-inch blossoms on 24-inch stems for midseason; 'Evergold,' bearing deep gold flowers on 40-inch stems and blooming in August; 'Ed Murray' with deep black-red flowers on 28-inch stems for midseason; 'Hyperion,' a fragrant, lemon lily blooming midseason on 42-inch stems; and 'Stella de Oro' with 2½-inch, golden-yellow flowers that bloom from late June into autumn.

Delphinium, Larkspur

Hosta, Plantain Lily

Delphinium species

Zone: USDA 4 to 6

The genus of this plant comes from the Greek word for "dolphin" and is suggested by the shape of a gland in the blossoms that secretes nectar. Many delphiniums are poisonous to cattle.

Description: The alternate leaves are cut and divided. Plants produce tall spikes of showy flowers, usually in shades of blue, each having a long spur behind the petals.

Ease of care: Moderately difficult

How to grow: Delphiniums are worth almost any effort to grow because they are so beautiful. They need full sun and a good, deep, well-drained, evenly moist soil that has a high humus content. If the soil is too acid, agricultural lime should be added. They are hardy feeders that must be supplied with compost or well-rotted manure, benefitting from feedings of a 5-10-5 fertilizer every year.

The area where they grow should have some protection from high winds because the hollow flower stalks, though strong, are often so covered with flowers that they can easily break in the breeze. Many gardens use delphiniums in front of stone walls for this reason. Without such protection, the gardener will have to resort to staking. After flowering, flower heads should be removed unless seeds are wanted. Surprisingly, these plants are very cold-hardy and resent hot climates and long, blistering summers.

Delphiniums are short-lived perennials that lose their vitality after two to three years. Since they grow easily from seeds and cuttings, propagation is not much of a problem.

Propagation: By cuttings, by seed, or by careful division.

Uses: Short delphiniums can be used in the front of a garden, the *Belladonna* hybrids in the middle, and the tall Pacific Coast hybrids in the rear. They are excellent cut flowers, too.

Related species: Only hardy to USDA 8, *Delphinium cardinale,* or scarlet larkspurs, are lovely flowers for the summer garden. *Delphinium elatum,* or the candle larkspur, is one of the sources for many of the most beautiful delphinium hybrids today. Reaching to 6 feet, the flowers are now available in white, lavender, blue, and purple. The Belladonna hybrids are light blue with 5-foot stalks and, if spent flowers are removed, they will usually produce blooms all summer long. 'Casa Blanca' is pure white. The Blackmore and Langdon hybrids were first developed in 1905. Today's plants bear pastel blue, lavender, white, violet, and indigo flowers on 4- to 5-foot stems. The Pacific Coast hybrids produce 7-foot stalks that must be staked even when given protection; the flowers in various shades of blue and pink are spectacular. 'Magic Fountain' is a dwarf version growing to 30 inches with double blooms. 'Connecticut Yankee' is a bush delphinium with single flowers of mixed colors on 30-inch stalks. *Delphinium grandiflorum* (sometimes called *D. chinensis*), or the Siberian larkspur, has finely cut foliage and blue flowers on 2- to 3-foot stalks, blooming the first year from seed if started early. 'Blue Mirror' has gentian-blue flowers and 'Alba' is white.

Hosta species

Zone: USDA 4

Next to daylilies, the most common garden perennial plants are the hostas. The original species came from Korea, Japan, and China where they have been cultivated for centuries. The Japanese grow them in deep shade and full sun in pots, gardens, rock gardens, and temple gardens. They even use them cut up in stir-fry.

In 1894, William Robinson called these plants *Funkia.* They were named in honor of Heinrich Christian Funck, a German doctor. By the turn of the century, the genus had been changed to *Hosta* in honor of Nicolaus Host, another German doctor. Both names still remain.

Description: Usually large clumps of basal leaves with pronounced veining and smooth or wavy edges distinguish hostas. Leaf colors come in various shades of green, often with many variegations. Lilylike flowers on tall stems (or scapes) in white and many shades of blue bloom from late spring to late summer.

Ease of care: Easy

How to grow: Hostas do best in good, well-drained, moist garden soil with plenty of humus. They require some sun to partial shade to deep shade, depending on the species and variety. Many hostas can take a great deal of sun and adapt to dry spots in the garden. They dislike wet soil in winter. Once in place, hostas can survive for generations. The plants are very tough and only slugs present a problem that, if left unchecked, can produce large holes in the leaves.

Propagation: By division or by seed (some species).

Hosta (continued)

Indigo, False; Wild Indigo

Uses: There is a place in every garden for hostas. The smaller types are excellent in the border or as ground cover. The larger varieties become elegant specimen plants forming gigantic clumps of leaves over the years. Although usually grown for the leaves, the flowers are often beautiful, too. Hostas are the backbone of the shade garden, since many of them are happiest in full or open shade protected from the rays of the sun. They are also excellent in pots.

Related species: Some hosta suppliers will stock well over 200 different species and varieties of this adaptable plant. The following list is only a sampling of what's available and the list grows every year. Those named enjoy shade to partial sun.

Hosta Fortunei forms mounds about 14 inches high and 2 feet wide with oval leaves 5 inches wide and 12 inches long with pale purple flowers in early summer. 'Albo-marginata' has a yellow-gold margin on a dark green leaf and 'Albo-picta' has a bright yellow leaf with a crisp, dark green margin. *Hosta lancifolia* has small, spear-shaped, dark green leaves about 6 inches long, forming clumps about 1 foot high and 18 inches wide. Flowers are light purple on 22-inch stems blooming in summer. *Hosta montana* has dark green leaves 11 inches wide and up to 20 inches long forming a mound 30 inches high and up to 4 feet wide. Flowers are off-white and bloom in early summer. 'Aureo-marginata' has wavy leaves of a glossy green with irregular, yellow margins. *Hosta plantaginea,* or the fragrant hosta, has large, heart-shaped leaves and produces sweet-smelling, white flowers in late summer or early autumn that can be killed by early frost if not protected. 'Grandiflora' has larger flowers in clumps that can reach 3 feet in diameter. *Hosta Sieboldiana* has round, blue-green, and seersuckered leaves 12 inches wide and 14 inches long in mounds that can reach 30 inches high and 4 feet wide. 'Frances Williams' has blue-green leaves with broad, golden-yellow margins that deepen in color

as the summer progresses. Lilac flowers appear in early summer. *Hosta Sieboldii* is a smaller plant with dark green, lance-shaped leaves a bit over 1 inch wide and 4 to 5 inches long. Flowers are white with purple veins and bloom in August. 'Kabitan' has leaves with a greenish-yellow base and a narrow, green margin. *Hosta undulata* has wavy leaves about 6 inches long and pale purple flowers in early summer. 'Variegata' has leaves with more white than green. *Hosta venusta* is a small plant from Korea with slightly wavy, green, heart-shaped leaves, 1 inch long and 1 inch wide. Flowers are violet and bloom in the early summer.

Baptisia australis

Zone: USDA 5

A beautiful plant in leaf, in flower, and after going to seed, false indigo was originally planted to produce a blue dye for early American colonists. Unfortunately, the dye wasn't fast. The name of the genus is from the Greek word for "dipping," which is also the root word for baptism.

Description: This is a large plant that grows to 4 feet in height. The blue-green, compound leaves on stout stems are attractive all summer and the dark blue, pealike flowers that eventually become blackened pods are very showy.

Ease of care: Easy

How to grow: It needs well-drained soil in full sun, but will accept some partial shade. Being a member of the legume family, baptisia will do well in poor soil. The root systems of older plants become so extensive that they become difficult to move.

Propagation: By division or by seed.

Uses: One baptisia will in time cover an area several feet in diameter with gracefully arching foliage. Because they die down to the ground in winter, a line of these plants makes a perfect deciduous hedge when spaced 3 feet apart. Because of the extensive root system, these plants are perfect for holding banks of soil in place. One plant makes a perfect specimen in the border. In addition, these plants are excellent for a meadow garden, a wild garden, or planted along the edge of the woods. The flowers are also beautiful when cut. After the fall frost, the leaves, as well as the inflated seedpods (often called Indian rattles) turn black. Expensive florist shops often gild these pods.

Iris

Iris species

Zone: USDA 4 and above

Related species: The prairie false indigo, *Baptisia leucantha,* has white flowers. It does well in the shade, although it is best in the wild garden since it's too rangy for a formal spot. *Baptisia perfoliata* is only reliably hardy to USDA Zone 7. The stems arch gracefully to the ground. The flowers are small and yellow, bloom in July, and appear surrounded by the gray-green leaves that resemble eucalyptus plants in growth habit. This plant is drought-resistant.

Just as gardeners could create a fascinating garden using nothing but daylilies and hostas, the same approach would also work for the iris. This large genus contains over 200 species in the northern hemisphere and is most abundant in Asia. The plants are responsible for a marvelous array of flowers plus, in many cases, fine foliage. In addition, some of the European species produce orris from the dried and powdered roots (or rhizomes), which has the odor of violets and is used for making perfume. The blue flags, *Iris versicolor* or *I. prismatica,* are lovely wildflowers of the Northeast, appearing in ditches and boggy areas along country roads. The crested dwarf iris, *I. cristata,* is another beautiful native iris perfect for the garden.

The genus *Iris* is derived from the ancient Greek word for "rainbow," referring to the many colors of the flower. The French heraldic symbol of the "fleur-de-lis" is thought to have been inspired by the hybrid German iris, *Iris germanica,* or the African yellow water flag, *I. pseudacorus.*

Description: Irises usually have basal leaves in two ranks, linear to sword-shaped, often resembling a fan, arising from a thick rootstock (or rhizome) or, in some species, from a bulb. There are three groups in the rhizomatous species: Bearded iris has a "beard" or pattern of hairs on the bottom half of the falls (the lower petals); the crested iris has a cockscomblike crest on the falls; and the beardless iris has no hairs on the bottom petals. They come in shades of pink, blue, lilac, purple to brown, yellow, orange, dark to almost black, and white. There are no true reds.

Ease of care: Easy

How to grow: Most irises need sunlight. Except for those like the water flag (*Iris pseudacorus)* that delights in a watery spot or the Japanese iris (*I. ensata)* that wants a humus-rich, moist soil, they also prefer a good, well-drained garden soil. In the North, rhizomatous irises should have the tops of the rhizome showing when planted; in the South, they should be covered slightly. The fan of leaves is to be pointed in the direction you wish the plants to grow.

Propagation: By division in the fall or by seed.

Uses: Even though bloom period is short, a bed of irises is ideal for a flower garden. There are irises for the poolside and the pool, the wild or woodland garden, the early spring bulb bed, and the rock garden.

Related species: The tall, bearded iris, hardy to USDA 4, sometimes called *Iris germanica,* usually comes to mind when people think of irises. The flowers come in a multitude of color combinations and sizes, with hundreds of new varieties introduced every year. The fanlike leaves are a lovely gray-green, browning at the tips in a hot summer. There are varieties that bloom both in the spring and the fall. Tall, bearded irises are over 25 inches tall; intermediate bearded ones are between 16 and 27 inches tall; the standard plants are between 8 and 16 inches; and the miniatures grow to 8 inches tall. As with daylilies and hostas, there is a bewildering number of varieties and colors. Perhaps the best suggestion for the beginning gardener is to order a mix of colors, a choice frequently offered by most nurseries.

Iris (continued)

Lady's Mantle

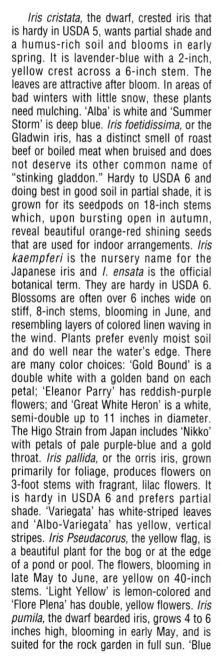

Iris cristata, the dwarf, crested iris that is hardy in USDA 5, wants partial shade and a humus-rich soil and blooms in early spring. It is lavender-blue with a 2-inch, yellow crest across a 6-inch stem. The leaves are attractive after bloom. In areas of bad winters with little snow, these plants need mulching. 'Alba' is white and 'Summer Storm' is deep blue. *Iris foetidissima,* or the Gladwin iris, has a distinct smell of roast beef or boiled meat when bruised and does not deserve its other common name of "stinking gladdon." Hardy to USDA 6 and doing best in good soil in partial shade, it is grown for its seedpods on 18-inch stems which, upon bursting open in autumn, reveal beautiful orange-red shining seeds that are used for indoor arrangements. *Iris kaempferi* is the nursery name for the Japanese iris and *I. ensata* is the official botanical term. They are hardy in USDA 6. Blossoms are often over 6 inches wide on stiff, 8-inch stems, blooming in June, and resembling layers of colored linen waving in the wind. Plants prefer evenly moist soil and do well near the water's edge. There are many color choices: 'Gold Bound' is a double white with a golden band on each petal; 'Eleanor Parry' has reddish-purple flowers; and 'Great White Heron' is a white, semi-double up to 11 inches in diameter. The Higo Strain from Japan includes 'Nikko' with petals of pale purple-blue and a gold throat. *Iris pallida,* or the orris iris, grown primarily for foliage, produces flowers on 3-foot stems with fragrant, lilac flowers. It is hardy in USDA 6 and prefers partial shade. 'Variegata' has white-striped leaves and 'Albo-Variegata' has yellow, vertical stripes. *Iris Pseudacorus,* the yellow flag, is a beautiful plant for the bog or at the edge of a pond or pool. The flowers, blooming in late May to June, are yellow on 40-inch stems. 'Light Yellow' is lemon-colored and 'Flore Plena' has double, yellow flowers. *Iris pumila,* the dwarf bearded iris, grows 4 to 6 inches high, blooming in early May, and is suited for the rock garden in full sun. 'Blue

Frost' has light blue flowers; 'Red Dandy' is a wine-red; and 'Golden Fair' is a deep gold. *Iris sibirica,* the Siberian iris, is a plant that has beautiful 3- to 4-inch flowers on 30-inch stems and great foliage—the sword-like leaves stand erect and eventually form a large clump. They need full sun, prefer a good, moist soil, and are hardy in USDA 4. 'Blue Brilliant' is as named; 'Ruffled Velvet' has deep plum-purple flowers; and 'Snow Queen' is pure white. *Iris tectorum,* the Japanese roof iris, is supposedly used as a living binding material for thatched roofs in the Orient. Plants are hardy in USDA 5; grow about 1 foot high; and are covered in June with 6-inch, lilac-blue flowers. Soil should be good and moist, with mulch used in areas without winter snow. 'Alba' is white.

Alchemilla species

Zone: USDA 3b

Lady's mantles are beautiful plants usually grown for their foliage and the unusual chartreuse flowers. The botanical name is a Latinized term for an old Arabic name.

Description: Plants grow between 8 and 14 inches high, with lobed leaves of gray-green that bear silky hairs.

Ease of care: Easy

How to grow: Lady's mantles are easy to grow in average garden soil where summers are cool and moist, preferring some protection from hot sun in mid-summer. In warmer parts of the country, they need a moist, fertile soil and light shade. As the summer progresses, the plants become larger and have a tendency to flop about. Flowers should be removed before the seeds ripen since they can seed about.

Propagation: By division in spring.

Uses: The flowers appear in clusters in early summer, standing well above the leaves, and last for several weeks. They are excellent when cut. These plants can be used in the front of the garden border or along the edge of a low wall where the leaves are easy to see.

Related species: Three species are usually offered: *Alchemilla alpina,* the alpine lady's mantle, grows about 8 inches high; *Alchemilla erythropoda* grows about 6 inches high; and *Alchemilla mollis,* the most common, grows to 14 inches high.

Lavender

Leopard's-Bane

Ligularia

Lavandula angustifolia
Zone: USDA 6

These are species of aromatic herbs originally from the Mediterranean. The genus name is from the word *lava,* which originally referred to a torrential downpour of rain and then became the word *lavare,* "to wash." It alludes to the ancient custom of scenting bath water with oil of lavender or a few lavender flowers.

Description: Plants are shrubby, usually with square stems and narrow, evergreen leaves that are white and woolly when young. Flower spikes have terminal clusters of lavender or dark purple flowers, blooming in late June and bearing a pleasing scent.

Ease of care: Easy

How to grow: Lavender plants want full sun and well-drained, sandy soil—preferably not acid. In areas where there is no snow cover, the plants should be mulched. In colder areas, prune back the dead wood in the spring.

Propagation: By soft cuttings in spring or by seed.

Uses: Lavender is perfect as a low hedge and in clumps next to rocks. It is also suitable in front of stone walls that face away from the wind.

Related varieties: 'Hidcote' has deep violet flowers on 20-inch shrubs; 'Munstead Dwarf,' a shorter type, has deep purple flowers at a 12-inch height.

Doronicum cordatum
Zone: USDA 5

All the plants in this genus were once thought to be poisonous to animals, hence the common name of "leopard's-bane." The genus is from an old Arabic name for the flowers. Some catalogs list it as *Doronicum caucasicum.*

Description: Bright, yellow, daisylike flowers bloom 2 inches across and reach a height of up to 2 feet. Leaves are heart-shaped with a toothed edge; they clasp the stems. Plants bloom in the spring.

Ease of care: Easy

How to grow: Leopard's-banes prefer a good, well-drained soil in partial shade. Since their roots are shallow, they also benefit from a moist situation. These plants prefer cool summers. In hot climates, they must have some shade.

Propagation: By division in early spring or by seed.

Uses: Since these flowers bloom in spring and usually go dormant by mid-summer, they should be planted where their absence will not be missed. They make fine border plants when massed and are beautiful in front of a low wall. They also make excellent cut flowers.

Related varieties: 'Magnificum' has larger-than-average heads and 'Finesse' bears bright yellow blooms 3 inches in diameter on 18-inch stems.

Ligularia species
Zone: USDA 4 to 6

The plant's name comes from the Latin word *ligula,* which means "little tongue," and refers to the tonguelike shape of the large petal on each of the ray flowers.

Description: Basal leaves on stout stems are either round or kidney-shaped. They bear tall spires of yellow or orange flower heads. The flowers smell of chocolate.

Ease of care: Easy

How to grow: Ligularias do best in partial shade and good, humus-rich garden soil that is kept evenly moist. Even with plenty of water, the leaves will wilt in hot summer heat, but they quickly recover as the sun sets and temperatures fall. Since the roots form large clumps, plenty of space should be allowed between plants.

Propagation: By division in spring or by seed.

Uses: Ligularias are great in the back of shady beds, along borders, in bogs, or planted at the edge of water gardens.

Related species: *Ligularia dentata,* 'Orange Queen' and 'Othello,' each have leaves up to 1 foot wide. The first is green throughout with flowers of a deeper orange, while the second has leaves that are green on top and purple underneath. *Ligularia przewalskii* 'The Rocket' and *Ligularia stenocephala* 'The Rocket' both bloom in late July and early August with large, serrated leaves and tall spires of bright yellow flowers on purple stems. *Ligularia tussilaginea* 'Aureo-maculata' has leaves splotched with areas of yellow or white. It is only hardy to USDA 7. *Ligularia veitchiana* forms large clumps that can reach 7 feet if growing conditions are good. Flower heads are bright orange and are about 2½ inches across.

Lungwort, Jerusalem Sage

Pulmonaria officinalis

Zone: USDA 4

One of the first flowers of spring, the lungworts are exceptional plants for both their blossoms and foliage. Because the leaves are dotted with white spots, the plant was thought to be a medicine for lungs. The genus name is from the Latin word for "lung."

Description: Lungworts have simple, basal leaves growing to 1 foot long, which are spotted with silver-white splotches. Terminal coiled clusters of 5-lobed flowers, which in many species open as pink and then fade with age to blue, bloom in the spring.

Ease of care: Easy

How to grow: While lungworts will persist in poor soil, they are truly lovely when planted in a good, moist garden soil in partial to full shade. Water must be provided during times of drought.

Propagation: Division in fall or by seed.

Uses: Lungworts are lovely plants for the shade garden, the wild garden, and even as ground covers on banks under the shadow of trees and bushes. Plants can be potted in late fall and forced into greenhouse bloom.

Related species: *Pulmonaria angustifolia* 'Azurea' is a European plant that bears brilliant blue flowers; 'Johnson's Blue' has gentian-blue flowers. *Pulmonaria montana,* often called *P. rubra,* has plain green leaves and bears salmon-red flowers. *Pulmonaria saccarata,* or the Bethlehem sage, is usually found with 'Mrs. Moon,' which has very attractive leaf spotting; 'Janet Fisk' has much silver on its foliage. 'Sissinghurst White' bears white flowers.

Lupine

Lupinus polyphyllus

Zone: USDA 5

Some authorities think that *Lupinus* comes from the Latin word for "wolf," since it was an ancient belief that lupines destroyed the fertility of the soil. Others, however, think the name is from the Greek *lype* for "bitter," because the seeds have a bitter taste and were considered a food of the downtrodden.

Description: Attractive, alternate, gray-green leaves are fingerlike, with many leaflets beginning at a central point. In early summer, plants produce 30-inch spikes of pealike flowers followed by silky seedpods.

Ease of care: Moderately easy

How to grow: Lupines require a lot of water and a spot in full sun or in the lightest of shade. Plants resent areas with hot summers. Soil must be well-drained with additional grit or sand. Lupines do not adapt to alkaline soil. Remove the dead flowers to prevent seed formation and to conserve the plant's strength. Cutting back to the ground after flowering will often produce a second crop of blossoms.

Propagation: By seed or division in early spring.

Uses: Lupines should be planted in large groups where their flowers make a spectacular sight. The plants are especially suited to seaside gardens.

Related varieties: The Russell strain of lupines is the variety that is usually offered by nurseries. They can be purchased in mixed colors that include blue, pink, red, purple, maroon, white, and mixed colors. Some nurseries also offer individual colors.

Obedient Plant, False-Dragonhead

Physostegia virginiana

Zone: USDA 4

A member of the mint family, obedient plants are native American wildflowers, still called *Dracocephalum* in some reference books. The genus name is from the Greek for "swollen bladder" and refers to the inflated body of the flower.

Description: Basal rosettes are evergreen in milder climates. Square, strong stems are from 1- to 3-feet tall and have narrow, toothed leaves, bearing rose-purple flowers that resemble a snapdragon. The individual flowers can be pushed around the stem without harm and will remain pointing in the direction when last touched.

Ease of care: Easy

How to grow: Plants like full sun and will tolerate most soils, preferring the addition of some organic matter. They are at their best in moist conditions. The common types are invasive and should be either fenced at ground level or divided every two years.

Propagation: By division in spring or by seed.

Uses: Because they flower late in the season, these are valuable plants for beds and borders. They will often bloom into October. They should be planted in groups and are excellent in the wild garden.

Related varieties: 'Alba' is pure white and blooms in late summer on 24-inch stems; 'Bouquet Rose' has rose-colored flowers on 3-foot stems; and 'Vivid' stays about 15 inches high with lavender-pink flowers.

Peony

Phlox, Garden

Paeonia species

Zone: USDA 5

Not only are peony flowers beautiful, the plants themselves are especially attractive. Throughout history, peonies have been famous—they have inspired poetry, been the subjects for tapestry and wall paintings, and included in witches' brews. They are named for the Greek physician Paeon, who was the first to use the plants for medicinal purposes.

Description: Herbaceous peonies are shrubby plants with thick roots and large, compound, glossy green leaves on reddish stems. They bear large, many petaled, showy flowers with a pleasing fragrance. They bloom in June and are followed by large, interesting seedpods. Ants are often seen in company with peony buds. Herbaceous peonies die down to the ground for the winter. Tree peonies have branches with obvious bark. Like a small tree, they remain in evidence all year and should not be cut down.

Ease of care: Easy

How to grow: Autumn planting is best. This means full sun (except in the South) and a proper hole with good, well-drained, moisture-retentive soil rich with humus. If soil is excessively acid, add one cup of lime per plant. Keep manure and added fertilizers away from direct contact with the roots. Plant with the "eyes" or growing points to the top about 1½ inches below the soil surface. Water well. Mulch the first year to protect from severe cold.

Propagation: By division of the roots or by seed (seedlings will take 3 years or more to bloom).

Uses: As specimen plants, in hedges, beds or borders, and even in the cutting garden, peonies should be an important part of any garden. Remember that even if they did not bloom, the attractive shape and gloss of the leaves and their shrubby aspect make them valuable.

Related species: *Paeonia Mlokosewitschii*, or the Caucasian peony, bears yellow flowers about 5 inches across. *Paeonia suffruticosa* is the Japanese tree peony (originally Chinese but refined—not discovered—by the Japanese), which is actually a bush, usually reaching a height of 5 feet and a spread of 6 feet. Flowers are between 6 and 8 inches across. 'Chinese Dragon' has semi-double blossoms of a rich crimson; 'Age of Gold' has large, double, golden blossoms; and 'Gauguin' has yellow petals inked with rose-red lines.

Related varieties: Various crosses of peony species have led to a large number of double varieties. According to type, they will bloom early, midseason, or late in June. Some of the more attractive are 'Bowl of Cream' with pure-white, double blossoms 8 inches across, blooming in midseason; 'Emma Klehm' has double, deep pink flowers that bloom late in the season; 'Coral Sunset' has flowers of intense coral, blooming early; and 'Sarah Bernhardt' has deep pink petals, lighter toward the edge with a marvelous fragrance, and blooms late in the season.

Phlox paniculata

Zone: USDA 5

Phlox are very popular plants since they are easy to grow, great for color, and marvelous for cutting. By far the most popular are the garden phlox and, over the years, a number of lovely kinds have been developed. The genus is named for the Greek word for "flame" and refers to some of the brightly colored flowers.

Description: Clump-forming perennials with very strong stems, phlox bear simple, lance-shaped leaves. These are topped with clusters of usually fragrant, showy, 5-petaled flowers arising from a narrow tube. They bloom over a long period.

Ease of care: Easy

How to grow: Garden phlox need good, well-drained soil in full sun or light shade, and plenty of water during the summer. Plants are often prone to powdery mildew. Keep individual plants 18 inches apart to promote air circulation. Divide plants every three years to keep them vigorous and deadhead to prolong bloom.

Propagation: By division or by seed.

Uses: Phlox can be bunched by color or mixed, the taller types best at the rear of the border.

Related species: *Phlox carolina* (once called *P. suffruticosa*) are native American flowers from North Carolina west to Missouri and then south, hardy to USDA Zone 5. They bloom from June into July. Soil should be good and well-drained in full sun. 'Miss Lingard' bears clear white flowers on 30-inch stems, while 'Rosalinde' has clear pink flowers on 36-inch stems, often blooming from late June into September. *Phlox divaricata*, or the wild sweet William, is another American native and a low-growing species, flowering in May and June. It prefers partial shade. Hardy to USDA Zone

Phlox (continued)

Pink, Carnation

Dianthus 'Constance Finis'

Dianthus species

Zone: USDA 5

4, plants usually bloom at a height of 14 inches. 'Fuller's White' has pure white flowers. *Phlox stolonifera,* or creeping phlox, is another native wildflower that crawls along the ground and bears purple or violet flowers on 6-inch stems in late spring. Plants are hardy to USDA Zone 4 and prefer light shade, but will take a half day of sun. 'Blue Ridge' has sky-blue flowers and 'Osborne's White' is pure white. *Phlox subulata,* or the mountain pink, is a creeping phlox used as a ground cover or in rock gardens, blooming in early spring. It is hardy in USDA Zone 4. Soil should be well-drained with full sun. Height is 6 inches.

Related varieties: 'Dodo Hanbury Forbes' is clear pink on 3-foot stems; 'The King' has deep purple flowers; 'Starfire' is a brilliant red; and 'White Admiral' is a pure white. All are on 30-inch stems. The Symons-Jeune strain of phlox was developed both for strength of stems and resistance to fungus—a problem that most of the phlox are susceptible to. Notable varieties are 'Blue Lagoon' with large heads of lavender-blue flowers on 40-inch stems; 'Dresden China,' flowers of a soft shell-pink on 4-foot stems; and 'Gaiety' with salmon blossoms with a cherry-red eye on 42-inch stems.

Pinks are the hardy flowers of the garden and carnations are usually thought of as being the flower of the buttonhole or the bouquet, although the terms are often mixed. Regardless of the name, these flowers are known for both their blossoms and for the marvelous sweet and spicy scent that many produce. The genus is a Greek word for "divine flower."

Description: Plants have narrow leaves on jointed stems that end with 5-petaled flowers with fringed edges, often having a distinct odor.

Ease of care: Easy

How to grow: Plants want full sun and a good, well-drained garden soil. Except for some of the alpine species, these plants are short-lived perennials and benefit by division every two or three years.

Propagation: By division, by cuttings, or by seed.

Uses: Pinks are excellent choices for a rock garden, hanging over the edges of a wall, or for the front of a garden, especially as edging plants. They make wonderful cut flowers and many will bloom all summer if spent flowers are removed.

Related species: *Dianthus barbatus,* or sweet Williams, produce clusters of varicolored flowers that are lovely in the border. They are thought of as biennials, but with self-seeding produce flowering plants year after year. *Dianthus deltoides,* or the maiden pink, forms low mats of leaves usually covered with delightful, single flowers on 6- to 12-inch stems perfect for the rock garden. It needs good drainage. 'Brilliant' bears bright, double crimson flowers. *Dianthus gratianopolitanus,* or the cheddar pink, produces clouds of flowers on 6- to 8-inch stems perfect for the rock garden.

The flowers are about 1 inch wide and beloved by butterflies. They are hardy in USDA 4. *Dianthus Knappii* comes from Yugoslavia and, unlike the other pinks in the clan, bears yellow flowers on 18-inch plants.

Related varieties: *Dianthus* X *Allwoodii* are hybrids produced years ago in England. The foliage is bluish-green with flowers of red, pink, or white, often with darker centers reaching a height of 18 inches. They must be divided every few years to survive. There are many cultivars available. 'Alpinus' is a dwarf growing up to 12 inches high; 'Blanche' is a glorious double white; and 'Robin' has bright red, double flowers.

Poppy

Rockcress

Rose, Christmas; Lenten Rose; Hellebore

Papaver orientale

Zone: USDA 5

Papaver is the ancient Latin name for the flowers and is thought to refer to the sound made in chewing the seeds.

Description: Basal leaves are covered with hairs. Graceful stalks grow to 4 feet and bear single or double flowers with petals of crepe paper texture surrounding many stamens. They flower in late May and June. Seedpods are attractive. Any part of the plant will bleed a milky sap when cut.

Ease of care: Easy

How to grow: Poppies are very undemanding, wanting only good, well-drained soil in full sun. Drainage is especially important in the winter as water will rot the roots. Place the crown 3 inches below the soil surface and mulch the first winter to prevent heaving. During heavy spring rains, try to cover the plant with Reemay cloth, a commercially available material that is very light and offers some protection. Plants go dormant in late summer, so their spaces should be filled with annuals or summer bulbs.

Propagation: By division in the fall or by seed.

Uses: Use poppies in beds or borders in combination with other perennials or in single groupings.

Related species: *Meconopsis cambrica,* or the Welsch poppy, has 4-petaled, orange or yellow flowers that close at night, adapt to light shade, and seed about the garden.

Related varieties: 'Carmen' bears brilliant red flowers; 'Harvest Moon' has flowers of orange-yellow; 'Lavender Glory' has deep lavender flowers with large, black, basal spots; 'Maiden's Blush' has ruffled petals of white with a blush-pink edge; and 'White King' is white.

Aubrieta deltoidea

Zone: USDA 5

Rockcresses are trailing perennials that usually burst into glorious bloom in late April and May. Plants originally come from Greece and Sicily. The genus is named in honor of Claude Aubriet, a French botanical artist of the 1700s.

Description: Rockcresses are creeping and trailing plants with small and simple leaves covered with tiny hairs. They bear a wealth of 4-petaled flowers, each about ¾-inch wide and typically in blues, lilacs, and purples. Plant height is between 4 and 6 inches. The leaves are evergreen when given snow cover, but turn brown without.

Ease of care: Easy

How to grow: Rockcresses prefer good soil with perfect drainage and a location in full sun. They will also do well in some shade and a very lean soil mix with a great deal of sand. After blooming is finished, they can be cut back.

Propagation: By division, by seed, or by cuttings.

Uses: Rockcresses are great for rock gardens where they form large carpets of bloom. They can also be planted in pockets of stone walls and do well in trough gardens. In addition, they are fine for the edging of borders.

Related varieties: 'Purple Gem' bears purple flowers on 6-inch stems; 'Bengel' produces larger-than-average flowers in rose, lilac, and deep red; 'Dr. Mules' is an old garden favorite with violet-purple flowers. 'Novalis Blue Hybird' is a new cultivar with a mid-blue color that comes from seed.

Helleborus species

Zone: USDA 4 to 5

Myth has it that an angel gave a Christmas rose to a young shepherdess that had no present for the Infant Jesus. The genus is an ancient Greek name for the plant. The entire plant is deadly poisonous.

Description: Deeply divided, usually evergreen leaves grow from a thick rootstock producing flowers with thick petals (really sepals) appearing in late fall, winter, or very early spring.

Ease of care: Easy

How to grow: Hellebores require good, deep, well-drained soil with plenty of humus and partial shade. When temperatures fall below 15° F, blooming is usually put off until the weather warms. At low temperatures, some protection is needed.

Propagation: By division or by seed.

Uses: The foliage alone is worth growing and makes an excellent ground cover. Flowers are good for cutting and the plants can be grown in pots or in a greenhouse.

Related species: *Helleborus niger,* or the true Christmas rose, bears white or pinkish-green flowers, and blooms in late fall, winter, or early spring. Although hardy in USDA Zone 4, winters often make growing difficult. *Helleborus orientalis,* or the Lenten rose, is the easiest of the species to grow, with cream-colored flowers fading to brown amidst palmlike foliage. This variety is also hardy in USDA Zone 5.

Related variety: 'Atrorubens' bears blooms in late winter or early spring with deep maroon flowers.

Sneezeweed, Swamp Sunflower

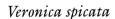

Helenium autumnale

Zone: USDA 4

There are many plants that begin blooming in early fall in bright colors that can often match those of autumn leaves. Sneezeweed is one such flower. The genus is from an ancient Greek word for a plant named after Helen of Troy. The common name refers to a profusion of golden pollen that could cause problems for allergy sufferers. They are native American plants.

Description: Small daisies have downturned, ray flowers on stout stems that branch toward the top and can reach 6 feet. Basal rosettes of leaves are evergreen in areas of mild winters. Plants bloom from late August through September.

Ease of care: Easy

How to grow: Although the plants are often found in dampish spots in the wild, swamp sunflowers can easily adapt to ordinary garden soil, especially in a low spot. During periods of drought, they need extra water. Nipping off the growing tips in the spring will help produce bushier plants.

Propagation: By division in spring or by seed.

Uses: Sneezeweed provides beautiful color for the back of a border or for an autumn or wild garden. They should be planted with ornamental grasses and with fall asters. They are excellent for cutting.

Related varieties: 'Riverton Beauty' has yellow flowers with a maroon eye; 'Butterpat' has flowers of clear yellow; and 'Moerheim Beauty' is bronze-red. All are on 4-foot stems.

Speedwell

Veronica spicata

Zone: USDA 5

Speedwell is a plant of the roadside with pretty flowers that "speed you well." In Ireland, a bit of the plant was pinned on to clothes to keep the traveler from accident. The flowers were named for St. Veronica.

Description: Plants have simple, oblong, 2-inch leaves usually opposite on strong stems. They grow to 18 inches, often bending, bearing densely branching spikes of small, blue or pink, 5-inch long flowers that bloom in summer.

Ease of care: Easy

How to grow: Speedwells will succeed in any good, well-drained garden soil in full sun or partial shade. Be sure to deadhead for repeat bloom. Plants will not usually survive wet feet in winter.

Propagation: By division or by seed.

Uses: The taller varieties are beautiful in both bed and border as well as in the rock garden. They are good cut flowers.

Related species: Veronica latifolia is usually available only as 'Crater Lake Blue,' with flowers of a deep gentian-blue on 18-inch stems. Veronica prostrata is a mat-forming type with deep blue flowers on 4-inch stems. 'Heavenly Blue' is usually offered.

Related varieties: 'Blue Peter' bears deep blue flowers in July and August on 24-inch stems; 'Icicle' is pure white on 18-inch plants; 'Minuet' has silvery green leaves and bears pink flowers on 1-foot stems in June; 'Nana' has blue flowers on 8-inch stems; 'Red Fox' blooms with deep rose-red flowers on 14-inch stems; and 'Sunny Border Blue' has violet-blue spikes that bloom from June until hard frost.

Spiderwort

Tradescantia x Andersoniana

Zone: USDA 5

Spiderworts are like daylilies and dayflowers—each blossom lasts only one day. The common name refers to the many glistening hairs on the sepals and the buds. They resemble a spider's nest of webs, especially when covered with dew ("wort" is an old English word for plant).

Description: Weak-stemmed plants with a watery juice and folded, straplike leaves grow up to 1 foot long. The 3-petaled flowers, open at dawn and fading by mid-afternoon, are surrounded by many buds.

Ease of care: Easy

How to grow: Spiderworts want good, well-drained garden soil in full sun or partial shade. In dry summers, they will need extra water. In too-rich soil, they grow quickly and tumble about. Even the newest types can become floppy by mid-summer—so when flowering is through, cut the plants to the ground and they will often flower again.

Propagation: By division in spring or by seed.

Uses: Although fine in the sunny border, the newer spiderworts are best in areas of open shade, especially under tall trees.

Related species: Tradescantia virginiana is the original species and is still found in many old country gardens. The flowers are usually 1 inch wide, violet-purple, and often very floppy.

Related varieties: 'Red Cloud' has deep, rose-red flowers; 'Zwanenberg' has very large, blue flowers; 'Snow Cap' is pure white; and 'Valor' is a deep red-purple. All grow to a height of 20 inches.

Stonecrop

Sedum spectabile

Zone: USDA 4

There are perhaps 600 species of these succulent herbs—mostly in the North Temperate Zone. Many make excellent garden subjects, but they are usually not found in most nursery centers and are only available from the various rock garden societies. The genus name is from the ancient Latin term, *sedere*, "to sit," referring to their low-spreading habit or possibly from *sedare*, "to quiet," alluding to their supposed sedative properties.

Description: Sedums have strong stems with succulent, usually alternate leaves. Terminal clusters of small, star-shaped flowers have 5 petals.

Ease of care: Easy

How to grow: Sedums need only a good, well-drained garden soil in full sun. They withstand drought and do amazingly well in very poor soils.

Propagation: By seed, by leaf cuttings, or by division.

Uses: The tall sedums, like *Sedum spectabile,* are excellent in the bed and border, especially effective when planted in masses. The shorter, sprawling types are best for the rock garden. Most make excellent cut flowers.

Related species: *Sedum Aizoon* reaches a height of between 12 and 18 inches with yellow to orange flowers in summer. *Sedum kamtschaticum* is only 4 inches high and has deep green, scalloped leaves. It bears orange-yellow flowers from July to September. *Sedum sieboldii* is often called the "October Daphne." It's a trailing plant with lightly scalloped leaves and lovely pink flowers appearing in late fall. Bloom is often killed by frost. *Sedum spurium* is a creeping sedum, evergreen even in Zone 5 and makes an excellent ground cover. 'Bronze Carpet' has leaves that are tinted bronze and bears pink flowers, while 'Dragon's Blood' has dark red flowers.

Related varieties: Probably one of the top ten perennials in the garden world today is 'Autumn Joy.' It is also known as 'Herbstfreude' or 'Indian Chief.' Although best in full sun, plants will take light shade. They are always attractive: Whether in tight buds of a light blue-green atop 2-foot stems; rosy pink in early bloom; in late bloom as the flowers turn mahogany; or a russet-brown during the winter. *S. spectabile* 'Brilliant' opens its flowers a month ahead of 'Autumn Joy'; 'Meteor' bears carmine-red blossoms on 18-inch stems; and 'Variegatum' has carmine flowers and leaves variegated with areas of creamy white.

Thistle, Globe

Echinops ritro

Zone: USDA 4

Globe thistles are large and stalwart plants for beds and borders that produce attractive balls of small, individual flowers. The genus name is in honor of the hedgehog because of the plant's prickly aspect.

Description: Globe thistles are 1½-inch balls of metallic-blue blossoms on stout, ribbed stems and, depending on the variety, grow from 3 to 7 feet tall. The leaves have spiny edges and are white-woolly beneath. They bloom in July and August.

Ease of care: Easy

How to grow: Globe thistles are not fussy as to soil and will do well in full sun or open shade. Once established, they are very drought-resistant. They seed about with ease.

Propagation: By division in the spring or by seed.

Uses: The larger species are impressive when used in background plantings or when grown as specimen plants. The smaller types are attractive in a bed or border or when spread throughout a wild garden. All look especially lovely when mixed with a planting of conifers.

Related species: *Echinops sphaerocephalus* is a species that is much taller, sometimes reaching 7 feet and best used where a strong statement is needed.

Related variety: 'Taplow Blue' has a more intense blue color in the flowers.

Wormwood

Artemisia 'Powis Castle'

Yarrow

Artemisia species

Zone: USDA 3

With the exception of *Artemisia lactiflora*, or mugwort, the rest of the wormwoods are best used for their foliage. The genus is named for the wife of Mausolus, an ancient king who built a giant tomb. Surprisingly, these plants are members of the daisy family and include sagebrush, common wormwood (the source of absinthe), and the herb tarragon.

Description: Wormwoods are shrublike plants usually with attractive silver-gray foliage and sprays of small, mostly unattractive flowers. The leaves and other plant parts are often aromatic.

Ease of care: Easy

How to grow: Plants prefer poor and sandy soils over deep and fertile earth. They must have full sun and good drainage or the roots will soon rot. Do not bother with these plants in areas of high humidity and damp summers. In warmer gardens, they can become weedy.

Propagation: By division or by seed.

Uses: The larger plants can be used as backgrounds to perennial borders; individual plants can be set about the garden to act as foils to bright and colorful blossoms, especially those with white, pink, or lavender flowers. When dried, they are excellent in winter bouquets.

Related species: *Artemisia abrotanum,* or southernwood, can be used as a deciduous hedge as it can grow to a height of 5 feet. *Artemisia Absinthium,* or common wormwood, has shiny, silvery, cut foliage on 4-foot stems. 'Lambrook Silver' has leaves of a finer cut. *Artemisia lactiflora,* or white mugwort, is the only one of this group grown for the flowers, which are not really white but more of a cream color. Masses of these tiny blossoms crowd 5-foot stems, starting in late summer and on into autumn. This plant needs better soil than the others. Even though the stems are strong, they might need staking in areas with gusty summer storms. They make excellent cut flowers. *Artemisia ludoviciana,* or white sage, bears willowlike leaves of silvery grayish-white on 3-foot stems. The variety *albula* has a cultivar 'Silver King' with beautiful foliage on 2-foot stems. *Artemisia Schmidtiana* 'Silver Mound' is a cultivar from Japan that grows in rounded balls with feathery, cut foliage about 20 inches wide. The mounds tend to spread with maturity and will eventually need to be divided. *Artemisia Stellerana,* or beach wormwood, is the only member to be somewhat inclined to humidity and is often found naturalized along sandy beaches of the Northeast. Plants grow about 2½ feet high with tiny, yellow flowers.

Achillea species

Zone: USDA 3b

Most people have seen the wild form of yarrow, *Achillea millefolium,* a wildflower originally from Europe and western Asia. The botanical name refers to Achilles, the hero of Greek legend, who is said to have used a species to heal battlefield wounds.

Description: Yarrow will grow between 1 and 3 feet high, blooming from June until August, and often until frost. Flowers are small and arranged in flat heads on top of stout stems. The foliage is finely cut and resembles a fern. Most species are aromatic and smell of camomile.

Ease of care: Easy

How to grow: Yarrows are especially valuable as they are tolerant of drought, suitable for any reasonably fertile garden soil that has good drainage. Plants revel in full sun, although they will tolerate a small amount of shade. New plants should be spaced about 12 to 18 inches apart.

Propagation: By division in spring or fall.

Uses: Yarrow are especially suitable for the garden border and look well in masses. They are excellent both as cut flowers and dried for winter bouquets.

Related species: 'Coronation Gold' bears large heads of golden-yellow flowers and is excellent for drying. The wildflower *Achillea millefolium* is suited for the meadow or wild garden; the cultivar *Achillea,* 'Crimson Beauty,' bears rose-red flowers on 2-foot stems; 'Moonshine' has sulfur-yellow flowers on 2-foot stems; *Achillea ptarmica,* 'The Pearl,' blooms with small, round, white flowers like its namesake on 3- to 4-foot stems. This plant has unbroken, weedy leaves.